A Season for the Spirit

A SEASON FOR THE SPIRIT

Readings for the Days of Lent

MARTIN L. SMITH

SEABURY CLASSICS
an imprint of
Church Publishing, Incorporated
New York, New York

A catalog record for this book is available from the
Library of Congress

ISBN 1-59628-006-9

Church Publishing Incorporated
445 Fifth Avenue
New York, NY 10016

CONTENTS

THE BEGINNING OF LENT

Ash Wednesday   The View From Jericho. 3
Thursday   In a Muddy River 7
Friday   The Wind in the Wilderness 11
Saturday   Finding the Spring 15

THE FIRST WEEK OF LENT

Monday   The Anesthetic Begins to Wear Off. 21
Tuesday   The Grief That Makes for Joy 25
Wednesday   I am a Little World? 29
Thursday   The Selves of the Self. 33
Friday   Each of the Faithful is a
   Little Church 37
Saturday   A Tree is Known by Its Fruit 41

THE SECOND WEEK OF LENT

Monday   Already 47
Tuesday   Rooted and Grounded in Love. 51
Wednesday   All the Dying 55
Thursday   No . . . and Yes 59
Friday   Everyone Enters the Kingdom
   of God Violently?. 64
Saturday   Body. 68

THE THIRD WEEK OF LENT
Monday Honor Your Father and
     Your Mother 75
Tuesday The One Who Desires 79
Wednesday The Wounded Child................. 83
Thursday The Child of Glory................. 88
Friday   The Repeat Offender 92
Saturday Those Other Christians 96

THE FOURTH WEEK OF LENT
Monday Domineering Virtues................ 103
Tuesday I Can Live With Mystery and
     the Unknown 107
Wednesday All the Sick....................... 111
Thursday Rejoice With Those Who Rejoice 116
Friday   Weep With Those Who Weep........ 120
Saturday The Burden-Bearer 125

THE FIFTH WEEK OF LENT
Monday You Always Have the Poor
     With You......................... 131
Tuesday Gifts Properly Affirmed 135
Wednesday The Doubters 139
Thursday Male and Female................... 143
Friday   Of One Blood 147
Saturday Widows' Mites, Living Stones 151

HOLY WEEK
Monday What We Know 159
Tuesday Pouring the Ointment 163
Wednesday Lying Close to the Breast of Jesus...... 168
Maundy Thursday If I Do Not Wash You............ 172
Good Friday Numbered With the Transgressors 176
Holy Saturday He Descended Into Hell............. 180

Endnotes 185
A Guide for Praying With Scripture 187

PREFACE TO THE CLASSICS EDITION

It is a strange experience for me as a writer to see the word "classic" linked with *A Season for the Spirit*. The book was originally commissioned by the then Archbishop of Canterbury, Robert Runcie, following the tradition that the leader of the Anglican Communion sponsors a Lent book every year. Such books usually remain in print only for a while and are soon replaced. I assumed the book—a devotional tool for readers in 1991—would be ephemeral. In fact, steady demand has kept it in print through the following years. I suppose if *A Season for the Spirit* continues to speak to thousands of readers year after year it has at least the *beginning* of a claim to be classic—so I tell myself. But the word classic suggests more than merely popular. Classic implies that the book has a more timeless character and a lasting authority, that it has transcended the limitations of a period-piece—and this is disturbing and humbling.

The nearest I can come to finding the claim justifiable is through my own experience of returning to *A Season for the Spirit* as a reader and a learner, rather than an author. Now I find myself in the ranks of readership, picking the book up not so much with the writer's complacent or critical review of his own handiwork, but in the expectation of having still a lot to learn from it, even wanting to use it again for my own life of prayer. Every writer knows what it is like to be surprised by what he is writing: Where is this coming from? Where is my authority to say such things? The mystery in writing, as with many of the arts, is that we learn from what we find ourselves making and much of it streams into our consciousness not from the storehouse of our own knowledge or experience but from beyond it. After the passage of time, this mystery can become even more impressive. Today I find myself as a learner and a seeker, reading and praying with the book again in order to listen to a wisdom in it that is far from being my possession.

Some of this classic wisdom is not so hard to trace. *A Season for the Spirit* is filled with quotations and allusions from classic voices of the Christian tradition. And where there is no direct quotation there is often an echo of the words of hundreds of men and women of the Spirit who have been guides and mentors to me over the years. This is the privilege of being a transmitter of a living tradition rooted in intimacy with God, and a willing participant in the communion of saints, all of whom are invested in our future, God's future, not in a bygone past.

A great twentieth-century lay Orthodox theologian, Paul Evdokimov, defined tradition as "something that is in accord with our future that we find in the past." Perhaps this gives us the clue to what a contemporary Anglican classic might be. It is a book that gives us resources of wisdom from the past that equip us to live authentically as people of our own time and inspires us to live under the authority of God's future.

Part of the reason for the appeal of *A Season for the Spirit* may be that it is helps us face the pluralism of our own era, a pluralism reflected in our experience of the complexity of being a person—a person with so many facets, so many "selves of the self." We need help to see how the mysterious presence we call the living Christ touches every person in the broken yet rich community that makes up every single human heart. We need help to see how the work of creating a community of love where there is room for everybody must be rooted in the exploration of our own inner fragmentation and diversity. A *Season for the Spirit* is offered again in the hope that many more may find some of that help as they pray with it.

February 2004

The
Beginning
of Lent

THE VIEW FROM JERICHO

Where do I stand at the beginning of another Lent?" Each one of us has a particular answer. I am at a certain point on a journey. Perhaps I have made progress since this day last year, wandered, or hung back. But the question also invites us all to make our annual pilgrimage to the same place, a certain common point for starting over again. The church gives us the map references for this place encoded in the gospels.

> In those days Jesus came from Nazareth of Galilee and was baptized by John in the Jordan. And just as he was coming up out of the water, he saw the heavens torn apart and the Spirit descending like a dove on him. And a voice came from heaven, "You are my Son, the Beloved; with you I am well pleased." And the Spirit immediately drove him out into the wilderness. And he was in the wilderness forty days, tempted by Satan; and he was with the wild beasts; and the angels waited on him. (Mark 1:9–13)

If I close my eyes I find myself at once standing at the vantage point for taking in the movement that the scripture describes, the swift movement of a young man leaving the river bank and Jericho.

When I set out for Jericho on a day in May 1973 my mind was full of memories of the lectures I had attended at Oxford given by Kathleen Kenyon, the archaeologist who had excavated it. But once I was there it was impossible to focus on archaeology.

Imagine yourself with me sitting in these ruins. We are looking south down the deepest cleft in the earth and in the distance the Dead Sea is shimmering in the intense heat like a lake of mercury. To the east the river Jordan snakes towards it, and the mountains of Moab from which Moses had seen the promised land tower beyond. To the west rise the massive brown hills of the wilderness, rent by deep gorges. Looking up towards the summit of the nearest mountain, Jebel Quruntul, we see an ancient monastery clinging to the cliffside.

This is the place where we are all invited to stand at the beginning of Lent to take in the meaning of this movement from the river to the desert, and to be caught up in it ourselves. Lent is the season for the Spirit of truth, who drove Jesus into the wilderness to initiate him into the truth that sets free. Mark's harsh word "drove" was softened by Matthew and Luke to the milder expression "led." But this word "drove" is very precious to me. I know that inertia, illusion, and fear hold me back from answering God's invitation to enter into the truth and gain freedom. Yet even Jesus, free as he was from inertia like mine, needed the full force of the Wind of God (Spirit, Breath, Wind are all equally valid translations of *pneuma*) to make him enter the testing-ground of the wilderness. If I am going to go forward into that truth for which God knows I am ready at this point in my life, I am going to need the Spirit to drive me.

This year I hiked in the deserts of southern Utah, and praying under the stars one night I smiled. Something I had seen that day had set me thinking about the vulnerability, the self-surrender of Jesus, giving himself over to the Spirit's driving force. I had seen some tumbleweed, matted thorns uprooted and rolled into a ball, bowled along unresistingly by the hot desert wind. The desert is a place of forces that cannot be resisted, flash floods and winds from which there is no escape. The forty days for Jesus began with this handing over of himself to the Spirit. "The wind blows where it chooses, and you hear the sound of it, but you do not know where it comes from or where it goes. So it is with everyone who is born of the Spirit" (John 3:8).

Perhaps this word "surrender" should be enough for my prayer on this Ash Wednesday. Not the surrender of submission to an enemy, but the opposite, the laying down of resistance to the One who loves me infinitely more than I can guess, the One who is more on my side than I am myself. Dwelling on this thought of letting go, and handing myself over to the Spirit will bring me much closer to the experience of Jesus than the word "discipline" that so many of us have been trained to invoke at the beginning of Lent. It should help us smile at our anxious attempts to bring our life under control, the belt-tightening resolutions about giving up this or taking on that. What we are called to give up in Lent is control itself. Deliberate efforts to impose discipline on our lives often serve only to lead us further away from the freedom that Jesus attained through surrender to the Spirit, and promised to give. "Where the Spirit of the Lord is, there is freedom" (2 Corinthians 3:17).

Lent is about the freedom that is gained only through exposure to the truth. And "What is truth?" Pilate's question is partially answered by unpacking the Greek word *aletheia*, which we translate as truth. The word literally means "unhiddenness." Truth is not a thing, it is rather an event. Truth happens to us when the coverings of illusion are stripped away and what is real emerges into the open. "When the Spirit of truth comes, he will guide you into all the truth" (John 16:13). The truth we are promised if we live the demands of this season consists not in new furniture for the mind but in exposure to the reality of God's presence in ourselves and the world. The Spirit promises to bring us into truth by stripping away some more of the insulation and barriers that have separated us from living contact with reality—the reality of God, of God's world, and of our true selves.

Spirit of truth, you know me intimately, you alone know what barriers to truth in me are ready to come down now so that I can enter more freely into the reality of God than ever before. Give me perseverance in my prayer and reflection day by day this Lent so that when the time is ready these barriers may give way like the walls of Jericho.

MEDITATION
Psalm 139   Joshua 6

Thursday

IN A MUDDY RIVER

If you were to picture the scene of Jesus' baptism in your imagination, what would it be like? What feelings would arise? I did not realize how much I had been influenced by the typical representations of the scene in conventional Christian art until I went to a showing of Pasolini's film *The Gospel According to St. Matthew.* I found myself taken by surprise at the scene of Jesus' baptism by John, and wept. It took a lot of thinking and praying to gain insight about why I had been moved by this scene in particular. In time I realized that hundreds of stained-glass windows and paintings depicted only the two figures in the water. But the film shook me into the realization that Jesus' baptism was not a private ceremony but a mass affair with hundreds of men and women swarming in the river, and hundreds more waiting on the bank to take their place. Religious pictures had blunted the impact of the gospels' insistence on the sheer numbers involved. "And people from the whole Judean countryside and all the people of Jerusalem were going out to him, and were baptized by him in the river Jordan, confessing their sins" (Mark 1:5). Luke repeats the word "multitudes" and paints the picture of a mass baptism: "Now when all the people were

baptized, and when Jesus also had been baptized…"
(Luke 3:21).

Insight gradually dawned that I had been moved by an
intuition of Jesus' solidarity with ordinary, struggling men
and women. John preached a "baptism of repentance for
the forgiveness of sins" (Mark 1:4). It was for the masses of
mediocre people whose failures, lukewarmness, and mun-
dane unfaithfulness made the prospect of coming judgment terrible. New converts to Judaism passed through a
baptismal rite as part of their initiation. Now everyone
needed a fresh start as radical as the one made by a pagan
who was embracing Judaism. John was offering to the
masses of ordinary people a baptism which could give
them that new beginning.

Jesus' reaction to John's preaching a baptism of repentance for the forgiveness of sins was a crucial turning-
point. He could have kept his distance, an innocent young
man conscious of unbroken faithfulness to God, looking
with pity on the thousands of ordinary people who were
overwhelmed by the realization of their own moral inadequacy. But instead of looking down on them from afar,
secure in his own guiltlessness, Jesus plunged into the
waters with them and lost himself in the crowd. He threw
away his innocence and separateness to take on the identity of struggling men and women who were reaching out
en masse for the lifeline of forgiveness.

It was at that moment when Jesus had thrown away his
innocent individuality in exchange for that identity of
needy, failed, struggling human beings that "the heaven
was opened, and the Holy Spirit descended upon him in
bodily form like a dove. And a voice came from heaven,
'You are my Son, the Beloved; with you I am well pleased'"
(Luke 3:21–22).

God's pleasure in Jesus can no longer be contained, and
it bursts out. God is well pleased precisely in Jesus' self-
emptying assumption of our identity. The Spirit reveals to
Jesus that he is the beloved Son of God at the precise moment

when Jesus had taken on the role of the Son of Man. The strange idiom that Jesus was to use to refer to himself might be better translated "the Human Being." In the muddy river Jesus was taking on the role of representing Humanity, of being its suffering Heart and Self before God. As soon as Jesus had done that decisively, God flooded him with awareness of his unique relationship as Son and anointed him with the life-giving Breath for his mission.

I had wept because the fleeting images of the film had invited me into the Jordan experience as no static stained-glass window or old master had done. Can you feel and see yourself as part of that crowd of humanity in the muddy water, as I started to then, and experience the entry of Jesus into our condition, into our needs? He chooses to plunge into it and make it his own. Nothing about me, about us, is foreign to him. He has chosen to be the Self of our selves.

And now, years later, I believe I wept because of the timing of the descent of the Spirit, the coincidence between the moment of Jesus' solidarity with human beings and the moment of God's revelation of intimate relationship with Jesus. Never did any event so deserve the name "moment of truth." The Spirit descended when Jesus embraced the truth of our interconnectedness, our belonging together in God. As soon as Jesus undertook to live that truth to the full, he was suffused with awareness of his own unique origin from and union with God and was filled with God's Breath. This coincidence reveals the axis on which the gospel turns. The barriers that hold us back from one another in fearful individuality are the identical barriers that block the embrace of God and insulate us from the Spirit. It is one and the same movement of surrender to open ourselves to intimacy and personal union with God in the Spirit, and to open ourselves to compassion and solidarity with our struggling, needy, fellow human beings. I was weeping in that Oxford cinema, though I did not understand this at the time, under the impact of this insight. To be open to the Spirit is also to be open to humanity in all its fractured confusion and poverty and its ardent reaching for fulfillment. To be open to the embrace of the Father is necessarily and inevitably to be open to the whole creation that is held in that embrace.

Spirit like a dove descending, in spite of my timidity I am appealing to you to center my heart on this axis of truth in these forty days. Every small step you enable me to take towards a deeper compassion for my fellow human beings will lead me further into the experience of the Father's delight in me and care for me. And vice versa. Every step I take in meditation to intensify my awareness of the love of God poured into my heart through the gift of your indwelling will take me into a deeper identification with the suffering world, "groaning in labor pains until now" (Romans 8:22).

MEDITATION
Romans 8:12–27

Friday

THE WIND IN THE WILDERNESS

L istening to others as a priest, as a friend, listening to the voices of my own heart and dreams, listening to everyone around me, I seem all the time to be hearing one or the other of two basic yearnings that gather up all the longings and hopes we have in common. One of these is the yearning to be joined with others, included with them. The other is the yearning to be distinct, unique, with an individual identity and integrity all one's own. I know I am constantly seeking to reconcile and balance these two yearnings and it appears that we all are. In the Jordan Jesus experienced a massive affirmation of uniqueness. He was the Beloved Son of God, the Anointed One. How would that experience fit with his sense of belonging to the crowd seeking forgiveness through John's baptism? If he is the Holy One of God, the Only-Begotten, what becomes of his sense of identification with weak mortals? Everything depends on whether Jesus can reconcile his sense of uniqueness as Son of God with his vocation as Son of Man to compassion and solidarity with needy, failed humanity.

So the Spirit like a dove descending suddenly becomes a gale that whips Jesus away from the throngs and drives him westward across the valley into the isolation of the desert. Being with others now would dissipate the energy needed to make this reconciliation. Only in silence and loneliness can he hammer out the question of who he really is.

His experience in those weeks of isolation and hunger will always be beyond our grasp. Their obscurity is pierced only by brief, enigmatic flashes; we are told that he was put to the test by Satan, entered the territory of wild animals, and was helped by the angels. Three snatches of dialogue with Satan hint that reconciliation between the two poles of Jesus' identity turned on the question of the use of power.

What was at risk was Jesus' solidarity with ordinary human beings. If he is the Son of God, why not use his prerogatives and miraculously provide bread for himself? The answer that rises from Jesus' depths is an answer about the human condition and the human vocation common to us all. Human beings cannot live by bread alone; they live on every word that God utters. Jesus needed to be one of these human beings and chooses to live in that precarious, day-by-day dependence on God's voice, which is the way for us all to live. To exploit miraculous powers would be to insulate himself from that dependence, and force him to part company with ordinary men and women struggling to be faithful to a hidden God.

If he is the Son of God, why could he not hurl himself from the parapet of the temple, confident of being protected from injury? To do so would be to force God's hand. Jesus rejects the suggestion as a horrible violation of simple trust in God. As he does so he deepens his identification with ordinary people who cannot afford to fool around challenging God to cushion them from suffering with sensational miracles. The common way of faith lives with a deep sense of vulnerability. By rejecting the way of spiritual bravado and the lure of invulnerability Jesus enters more deeply into his—our—humanity.

If he is the Son of God, why not simply take power? Jesus recognizes that to rule would be for him precisely to go over to the side of evil. Political mastery tears human solidarity apart by elevating the masters and forcing others into subservience. The glory of charismatic leadership depends on sustaining the illusion that the leader is above and beyond the common masses, an illusion they need as much as he or she does. From deep within Jesus emerges his refusal of the way of power, a refusal he will have to repeat again and again on the way to the cross. His vocation is to be the Servant, he will be "numbered with the transgressors," not the rulers. He will be unbreakably, doggedly, passionately one with God's struggling and needy children. To stand with them means he may never stand over them. He will not get into the position of receiving from his sisters and brothers any of the honor due to their Father alone. Later on he will even contradict a well-meaning man who calls him good. "Why do you call me good? No one is good but God alone" (Mark 10:18). Not even a single compliment will be allowed to pass if there is any risk of it diverting attention from the One who is all in all, or of compromising Jesus' solidarity with the masses of men and women who have failed to be good.

In Dorothy L. Sayers's novel *Gaudy Night* one of the characters recalls "the extempore prayer of a well-meaning but incoherent curate, heard once and never forgotten, 'Lord, teach us to take our hearts and look them in the face, however difficult it may be.'"[1] Taking our hearts and looking them in the face is the essence of the wilderness experience. It does not require sand and rocks, only sufficient silence for us to become aware of what we really feel, in the words of poet Matthew Arnold, "below the surface-stream, shallow and light of what we say we feel." A desert monk once asked a novice to took into a bowl of water, which he shook. When he stopped the agitation the novice could see the reflection of his face. In the stillness of the desert Jesus looked into his heart and saw how his sense of specialness as the Anointed could be distorted into a demand to be exempt from hardships and to have control over others. His surrender to the Spirit allowed him to break through to the truth that his specialness as the Beloved Son gave him the freedom to take human suffering upon himself and to be the Servant of all.

Spirit of Jesus, give me the courage to take my heart and look it in the face! It is absurd to be surprised to see there cravings to be special, to be invulnerable, to dominate. Only if you deepen my awareness of your indwelling and the priceless gift of intimacy with the Father which is already mine can these desires give way to the truth that I belong to others and can serve and embrace them.

MEDITATION
Luke 4:1–15   Matthew 4:1–23

Saturday

FINDING THE
SPRING

The image of the Spirit as wind driving us towards places where we will be exposed to liberating truth is an essential one, but it is only an image. If it became fixed and exclusive it would cease to be transparent to the mystery and would start to hinder us. Winds blow upon us from afar. But the Spirit is within us, and the place of encounter with our truth is not found on any map—it is within our own hearts. We cannot surrender to the Spirit or make our way to that place where truth can happen until an essential shift takes place in our consciousness and we realize that the meeting place with the Spirit is within our own selves. I will never forget the way that shift began to take place in my own experience.

In the last months of my schooldays I was pursuing my interest in local history by investigating the therapeutic wells and springs of Worcestershire. In my research I came across an account of an Edwardian expedition to discover a holy spring, in the vicinity of White Ladies Aston, I believe. In the Middle Ages, pilgrims with eye diseases had gone there to seek healing. All trace of it was lost and that expedition had been a failure. One warm day I strapped a spade to my bicycle and set out to see whether I could find it.

Nothing came of hours of probing in the fields where tradition located the spring, until I realized that the cows that stood in a stinking mud patch might be guarding the secret. I prodded them with my spade, forcing them to leave, and began to dig in the dung. After twenty minutes my spade grated against stone and moments later I had uncovered a carved platform from which protruded a wooden pipe. Pure water poured out in a steady flow. I had found the well, the place of pilgrimage and healing.

The deep sense of satisfaction and wonder I felt grew over the months that followed. Then when I read the fourth and seventh chapters of John's gospel I experienced a kind of enlightenment:

> The water that I will give will become in them a spring of water gushing up to eternal life. (4:14)

> On the last day of the festival, the great day, while Jesus was standing there, he cried out, "Let anyone who is thirsty come to me, and let the one who believes in me drink. As the scripture has said, 'Out of the believer's heart shall flow rivers of living water.'" Now he said this about the Spirit, which believers in him were to receive. (7:37–39)

I knew enough Greek to know that the word translated "heart" literally meant guts, the viscera, the womb. The old translation "belly" conveys the earthiness of the original. The home of the Spirit is not in the intellect, the realm of concepts and ideas, not in a refined interior *sanctum* of spirituality, but in the guts, the deep core where our passions have their spring, the place of conflict, confusion, vulnerability, and desire.

The fastidious Edwardian ladies and gentlemen had failed to find the spring because they had hurried past the stinking mud patch, the huddled beasts and swarming flies. I realized that we pass over the place of the Spirit's indwelling, that unpromising and murky place of our own guts, in just the same way, and look in vain for the Spirit in the cleaner world of thought and piety.

We have all heard the story of the man who was seen searching for something at night under a street light. "Did you lose something here?" he is asked. "No, over there," he replies, pointing to a dark corner some distance away, "but this is where the light is good." It is the story of the spiritual quest of so many of us.

So the Spirit is to be found in the core of our own humanity. One of the wonderful things about my discovery of the spring was the sense that it had been there, flowing, all the time, for centuries. It just needed to be uncovered. I knew God was teaching me about my own baptism in this experience. The Spirit had been in me all the time. Finding the Spirit of God in my life was not a matter of looking for something I had never had. It was a matter of actively uncovering through faith a Presence in the depth of my being that had been there all along, and that had been at work in my actions and sufferings, my fears and desires.

This active uncovering still goes on in prayer and I return again and again to the image of "the spring of water gushing up to eternal life" in my body. I remind myself that there, *there*, the Spirit "helps us in our weakness: for we do not know how to pray as we ought, but that very Spirit intercedes with sighs too deep for words. And God, who searches the heart, knows what is the mind of the Spirit, because the Spirit intercedes for the saints according to the will of God" (Romans 8:26–27).

Spring of life, I can only truly surrender to you if I recognize that you flow in me. If I call upon you from afar or worship you at a distance I am still evading the terrible and wonderful truth that you have made your home within my depths. I need to learn from the first page of scripture that you belong over the face of the waters of chaos, that you are the shaper, the reconciler, the healer, the consecrator through grace of the forces of our nature. I need to dare to worship and love you where you are—in my self, that is (if I am true to the words of Christ) in my gut, in my womb. Give me the courage today, not to look up to you but to look steadily within myself, and adore you there supremely at home where there is so much brokenness.

MEDITATION
John 4:1–15

On the last day of the festival, the great day, while Jesus was standing there, he cried out, "Let anyone who is thirsty come to me, and let the one who believes in me drink. As the scripture has said, 'Out of the believer's heart shall flow rivers of living water.'" Now he said this about the Spirit, which believers in him were to receive; for as yet there was no Spirit, because Jesus was not yet glorified.

John 7:37–39

The
First Week
of Lent

Monday

THE ANESTHETIC
BEGINS TO
WEAR OFF

If I give the image of the spring in the heart time to develop within my imagination, if I dwell long enough on the scriptures that teach about the indwelling of the Holy Spirit so that I begin to experience myself newly centered on the reality of this presence, I do not necessarily begin to feel glad about this. In fact the sure sign that the truth of it is really dawning for the first time is that I become uncomfortably aware of reluctance, even hostility. Many people who have been brought up as Christians relegate the mystery of the indwelling Spirit to an attic where they store teachings that common sense dictates to be implausible, "mystical," remote from reality. As soon as we allow ourselves to be grasped by the truth of it, the indifference we used to show is unmasked as actual resistance that tries to keep the Spirit at arm's length.

It is unnerving to reckon with a life active and powerful at work in the most intimate core of our beings, with access to inner rooms from which our own conscious minds are barred. One of the signs then that the truth of the Spirit's presence is beginning to make itself known is that we feel as if, in Paul Claudel's colorful words, "an undesired lodger has moved in, one who does not hesitate to rearrange the chairs according to his taste, to drive nails into the walls and, if necessary, even to saw up the furniture when he is cold and needs a fire."[1]

The truth of the Spirit's indwelling is incompatible with my sense of autonomy, my complete ownership of myself. To admit that the Spirit lives and moves within and throughout my whole self is to lose proprietorship of myself. I even have to surrender ownership of my prayer. I pray yet what I pray and how I pray is merely the tip of the iceberg of the prayer that goes on in me. The Spirit prays within me "with sighs too deep for words" and communicates with the Father at a deeper level than consciousness. Consequently, I can no longer assess the value of my own prayer with any confidence. My most fluent and satisfactory prayers may be the least effective in the eyes of God. The struggling, dry, inarticulate prayers I am tempted to denigrate may be the most powerful and authentic because they are welling up from the subliminal stirring of the Spirit.

The Spirit drove Jesus into the wilderness after descending upon and into him. What corresponds to this in our lives is the disorientation and loss of control we experience on realizing that the Spirit is alive and active at the core of our beings. We enter the wilderness in the sense that we lose our familiar landmarks, the criteria we habitually used to judge which of our feelings are valuable and which useless or shameful. We realize that if the Spirit is shaping and redeeming and empowering and purifying us from within, most of the judgments we make about the movements of our heart run the risk of being hasty and crude. Now the important thing is not to try to run our lives by conventional criteria but to suspend judgment and patiently listen to our own feelings and experiences so that the Spirit can reveal what is going on.

How can we tell what is coming from the Spirit within? We look for the signs within us of the same movements that Jesus experienced. If it is the Spirit of *Jesus* within us we will be able to recognize two movements. First, we will experience the Father moving to embrace us: "You are my beloved son, you are my beloved daughter." The Spirit of Jesus reproduces within us the experience of Jesus in the Jordan. Second, we will be impelled to embrace the suffering world in compassion. The Spirit of Jesus moves us, as it moved him, to identify ourselves with a broken world and to bring it within the reconciling embrace of God. Intimacy with God, identification with the fallen creatures of God, always both.

If the Spirit is to get us to experience—not just to think—these two movements, there is a primary obstacle to overcome. This is our habitual condition of being under an anesthetic. Most of us have a primary defense mechanism against being overwhelmed by the pain of the world and our own pain. It is as if we administer to ourselves an anesthetic to numb its impact. The price we pay is that it also numbs our capacity for joy, but until we surrender to the Spirit of God we reckon the price to be worth it. The strongest sign of the Spirit working within us is simply that the anesthetic begins to wear off. We start to come round and become vulnerable not only to the experience of joy at being found, embraced, and indwelt by God, but also vulnerable to pain, our own stored up pain and the pain of the world.

Experience of the Spirit of Jesus always has a paradoxical, twofold character. There is always joy and pain. Joy at our undeserved embrace by love, and the hope of being completely healed. Pain in sharper empathy with the suffering of a world which is so very far from being unified and healed in God.

When we cry, "Abba! Father!" it is that very Spirit bearing witness with our spirit that we are children of God, and if children, then heirs, heirs of God and joint heirs with Christ.... We know that the whole creation has been groaning in labor pains until now; and not only the creation, but we ourselves, who have the first fruits of the Spirit, groan inwardly. (Romans 8:15–17, 22–23)

Spirit who filled Jesus, no wonder I shy away from the mystery of your indwelling! The moment I consent to your living and moving in me, and trust you, the numbness I have relied on to get through life begins to wear off. Give me the faith to be vulnerable to the joy the Father has in me through my union with Jesus the Beloved. Give me the courage to share the pain of the world which is so far from its home and center, the Living God.

MEDITATION

Do you not know that your body is a temple of the Holy Spirit within you, which you have from God, and that you are not your own?

1 Corinthians 6:19

Tuesday

THE GRIEF THAT MAKES FOR JOY

The experience of the Spirit is joyful and painful because the light of "God's love...poured into our hearts through the Holy Spirit that has been given to us" (Romans 5:5) inevitably shows up our own poverty. Contrasted with the all-embracing scope of God's love, our own is exposed in all its narrowness and selectivity. As we experience ourselves wrapped around with a love that takes no account of deserving, from a God who "makes his sun rise on the evil and on the good, and sends rain on the righteous and on the unrighteous" (Matthew 5:45), we are made to recognize how far we are from extending that same generosity to the world around us, how far we have yet to go before we love our enemies.

This dual experience of painfully seeing ourselves so poor in love, and yet forgiven, is at the heart of what the ancient spirituality of the church called compunction. Compunction is a rather archaic word, seldom heard in current speech, though I heard it often as a child in a village school in the north country where many old expressions were still in common use. Perhaps it is worth preserving this unusual word because the movement in the heart to which it refers is not commonplace. Compunction is utterly different from remorse. There is no room in true compunction for self-loathing and the indulgence of lashing ourselves with blame. Compunction always arises from the knowledge that one is loved and forgiven, and the piercing (that is what the Latin root means) is of our complacency and self-justification. We know how far our conversion still has to go before we have an all-embracing love like God's. St. John of the Ladder, one of the great figures in early monastic spirituality, coined the classic definition of compunction, "the grief that makes for joy."

Compunction does not keep us raking over the failures of the past, fascinated by our sins. The Spirit turns us to the future, a future in which our hearts will be transformed so as to be as hospitable as the heart of God. Compunction turns us towards the prospect of being fully converted and warms our desire for it. Grief at our own poverty in mercy opens us towards the future gift of God in which the beatitude "Blessed are the merciful" will apply to us.

On Ash Wednesday we took our bearings for Lent from a vantage point where we could see in our imagination the movement of Jesus from the river to the desert. I mentioned the monastery that can be seen from Jericho, clinging to the side of the mountain to the west. Why did these men and women of the early monastic movement make their home in the wilderness of Jesus' temptations? One of the primary motives at the heart of the monastic impulse was the urge to discover the secret of Christ's limitless compassion. Men and women who knew themselves to be sustained by God's compassion, yet so lacking in mercy, made the experiment of going where Christ had been driven to enter into the same experience that had opened his heart to the full. The constant theme of the stories, the poems, and the teachings that flowed from the desert monasteries and hermitages was the attainment of a merciful heart. These words of Isaac the Syrian sum up a tradition of centuries of exploration:

What is a merciful heart? A heart which burns for all creation, for human beings and birds and animals and demons, and for every creature. As he calls them to mind and contemplates them, his eyes fill with tears. For the great and powerful compassion grips the heart and from long endurance his heart diminishes, and cannot bear to hear or see any injury or any tiny sorrow in creation. That is why he constantly offers prayers with tears for dumb beasts, and for the enemies of truth, and for those who hurt him, that they may be protected and shown mercy; likewise he prays for the race of creeping things, through the great compassion which fills his heart, immeasurably, after the likeness of God.[2]

The Arab name for the mountain above Jericho where the monastery is built into the side of the cliff, Jebel Quruntul, means "Mountain of the Forty Days" and it derives from the Crusaders' French word for Lent. If we take our bearings for our own Lent from this ancient monastic outpost we will once again be pointed in the direction of the quest for a breakthrough to solidarity. The spiritual quest is not for interesting "spiritual experiences" but for the expansion of our capacity for mercy, the opening of our hearts wide enough to embrace the world, and not just the fragments of it, here and there, which at present we manage to feel with and care about.

✎

Spirit of God, have I ever felt true compunction? Regret, remorse, self-criticism, deploring my failings—all these I know. But as I struggle now to be truthful I realize that there is often a self-centeredness in these feelings and little joy. There is a secret pleasure in wounding my self-esteem further with blame. But where is the joy at being forgiven, the pain of facing the pal-

*triness of my compassion, and the joy again of looking forward
to my own full conversion? These can only come as your gift.
No effort of mine can generate the "grief that makes for joy."*

*Today I desire to make a new start. In my self-examination
let me not lose myself in the contemplation of my own inade-
quacies. Let me lose myself in the contemplation of the all-
inclusive embrace of God's love in which I am held. Only then
will I be able to bear that pain of being shown how little I reflect
that mercy in my own life. Only then will my desire to have a
merciful heart be kindled.*

MEDITATION

> Mercy and just judgment in one soul is like a man
> worshiping God and idols in the same house. Mercy
> is the opposite of just judgment. Just judgment is the
> equality of equal measures: for it gives to each as he
> deserves.... Mercy, however, is pity moved by race
> and inclines to all in compassion.
>
> *Isaac the Syrian*

When Jesus saw the crowds, he went up the mountain; and after he sat down, his disciples came to
him. Then he began to speak, and taught them, saying: "Blessed are the poor in spirit, for theirs is the
kingdom of heaven. Blessed are those who mourn,
for they will be comforted. Blessed are the meek, for
they will inherit the earth."

"You have heard that it was said, 'You shall love
your neighbor and hate your enemy.' But I say to
you, Love your enemies and pray for those who per-
secute you, so that you may be children of your
Father in heaven; for he makes his sun rise on the
evil and on the good, and sends rain on the righteous and on the unrighteous. For if you love those

who love you, what reward do you have? Do not even the tax collectors do the same? And if you greet only your brothers and sisters, what more are you doing than others? Do not even the Gentiles do the same? Be perfect, therefore, as your heavenly father is perfect."

Matthew 5:1–5, 43–48

Wednesday

I AM A LITTLE WORLD?

"You yourself are even another little world and have within you the sun and the moon and also the stars."

These words come from a homily of Origen, one of the great pioneers of early Christian theology. The vision of the human person as a microcosm (a word meaning miniature world) is one of the most universal of religious insights. By my bedside is a reproduction of a scroll by a Zen monk of the seventeenth century, a great calligrapher named Tetsugyu. The translation of the characters is "Self revealed: all things in heaven and earth exist in oneself." It is the first thing I see when I wake up, and the last before I fall asleep; such is the importance it has for me.

Many of the men and women who went into the desert to discover what the Spirit could do there to expand and convert their hearts must have known of this ancient teaching, but they were not interested in philosophical speculations. It was experience that taught them that they did not leave the world to go into the desert. They took it with them. Far from society, alone, they experienced within themselves all the feelings, passions, yearnings, nightmares, and compulsions that made human society so precarious, so turbulent, so fractured. In the silence they heard many voices within themselves, as many as argued and struggled in the world. But it was not just human society that they discovered to be encapsulated within their own selves, but heaven too, with Christ at the center, present by the power of the indwelling Spirit. Alone, they were far from alone, their hearts the arena of a redemptive struggle between the Lord and his angels and the forces of disintegration and death.

The discovery that "all things are there" within the human heart is one of the great themes of desert preaching:

> Within the heart are unfathomable depths. There are reception rooms and bedchambers in it, doors and porches, and many offices and passages. In it is the workshop of righteousness and of wickedness. In it is death; in it is life.... The heart is Christ's palace: there Christ the King comes to take his rest, with the angels and spirits of the saints, and he dwells there, walking within it and placing his Kingdom there.... The heart is but a small vessel: and yet dragons and lions are there, and there poisonous creatures and all the treasures of wickedness; rough uneven places are there, and gaping chasms. There likewise is God, there are the angels, there life and the Kingdom, there light and the apostles, the heavenly cities and the treasures of grace. All things are there.[3]

This great insight that the whole world is mysteriously summed up in my own self, that I am God's world in miniature, is a great gift. With its help I can begin to understand the connection between God's love for the universe and God's love for each person.

The love God has for me is not an infinitesimal fraction of his love for the world. I do not get a tiny bit of his attention and care. Because the whole is present in each part, because I am the world in miniature, God is wholly present to me, wholly available. I receive myself the full force of his love for creation, and undivided attention and presence.

"God so loved the world that he gave his only Son, so that everyone who believes in him may not perish but may have eternal life" (John 3:16). God so loved the world, and God so loves each single person, in whom all the world is present in miniature. "The life I now live in the flesh I live by faith in the Son of God, who loved me and gave himself for me" (Galatians 2:20). Christ gave himself wholly for the world, and gave himself wholly for you and for me.

The monks and nuns who went into the desert where the Spirit had driven Jesus stayed there to learn that they were united to all the world, because all that is in the world was within each one. They stayed there to experience the absolute and undivided love of God embracing them, to experience in their own selves the full force of God's redemptive presence and activity.

You are not in the desert, you are going about your normal life. But Christ has asked you to be solitary for your prayer. "But when you pray, go into your room and shut the door and pray to your Father who is in secret." Worship together is important, praying while we move about during the day is important, but there is something essential in finding ourselves alone. Alone, behind closed doors, we face a moment of truth. There is an unspoken question in the air. Is God there for me? Is God's attention absorbed by the vast world, the need of the billions of God's other children? Faith falters and we scarcely dare "bother God" with our little needs. Only by persevering with this appearing before God alone can we come to know that the Father who sees in secret, secretly sees the whole world in each one of us and loves it, and cares for everything about us and in us.

Holy Spirit, it will take some leading on your part before I can accept this strange insight, that God, looking at me, sees the whole world in a nutshell. It has become second nature with me to think of myself as an individual who is just an infinitesimal particle in the world. What difference do I make? I am one face in an immense crowd, and worse, sometimes merely a number. What a revolution in my self-understanding would have to take place if I thought of myself as a microcosm, containing within myself all the elements that make human society so diverse, so conflicted, so rich! How differently I would pray! I can only begin to imagine what I would find myself praying. Perhaps something along these lines: "Father, I come to you knowing that I do not just get part of your attention, but all of it. As you look on me, you see the whole world condensed in my heart, a world in need of healing and reconciliation. You see your Son at my center. You love him, me, the world he is saving all in one. Help me experience this love in all its force." Holy Spirit, is this the kind of praying you want to teach me?

MEDITATION

The measure of his love to each is as great as the whole world.

St. John Chrysostom

Thursday

THE SELVES OF
THE SELF

Few people give us much encouragement to ask ourselves questions as basic as "Who am I?" We are expected just to carry on carrying on; we have no business indulging in such introspection. The spiritual life can only thrive by defying these prohibitions and the saints encourage ordinary people to take time to ask extraordinary questions. Here I am today asking myself who I am and wondering whether the ancient image of the self as microcosm will help me grasp the secret of becoming a more compassionate person, more expressive of the hospitality of God. If the image is valid it should at least throw some light on my experience of diversity within myself. Are there in fact many voices to be heard within myself, many selves to be encountered?

As soon as I start a dialogue with myself the reality of the self as a kind of society becomes apparent at once. I ask myself a question. So there are two selves for a start, one asking and one being asked! It takes two to have a dialogue. We continually address ourselves, our selves. When we encourage ourselves, there is a courageous self and a timid self in conversation. When we blame ourselves, there is a moral self accusing a self who failed. Sometimes these other selves belong to the past. Memories of past behavior can fill us with pride or loathing, and we congratulate or abominate the self we once were and that lives on within us. Or we find ourselves feeling and acting in ways that stem from experiences of long ago but are out of keeping with the present situation. It is as if the selves we once were linger on within and have power to seize the reins from time to time.

I experience more selves when I become aware of inner conflict around decisions. One voice beckons me in one direction, then another speaks in contradiction, luring me in another. The sense of inner dividedness can be bitter. In the words of e. e. cummings:

so many selves (so many fiends and gods
each greedier than every) is a man
(so easily one in another hides;
yet man can, being all, escape from none)
so huge a tumult is the simplest wish;
so pitiless a massacre the hope
most innocent (so deep's the mind of flesh
and so awake what waking calls asleep).[4]

When we sleep a whole cast of characters emerge from hidden places within to enact the dramas of the night. In our dreams we act without the restraints of the day or logic, with savagery, erotic passion, heroism. We meet odd characters, monsters, figures of grace and beauty, the maimed and the magnificent. Who are these figures? The more we attend to them and meditate on our dreams, the more meaning seems to be yielded if we regard the personages of our dreams as aspects of our own selves. When we, whose lives are often seemingly uneventful, emerge from sleep just having killed someone in a nightmare, or flown to the rescue of a drowning child, it is hard to deny the ancient insight that everything human can be found within one's own heart.

Personhood is so precarious that awareness of being one's self can disintegrate and leave only the sense of chaotic multiplicity. The strange story of Jesus' exorcism of the lunatic who lived in the graveyard of the Gerasenes comes to mind. "Then Jesus asked him, 'What is your name?' He replied, 'My name is Legion; for we are many'" (Mark 5:9).

The Holy Spirit of God dwells in your heart and is no stranger to the diversity and conflict there. The Spirit dwells with and among and between all the selves of your self. There is no secret place where the Spirit has no access, nor any inner person excluded from the Spirit's presence. What then does the Spirit want to do with all the selves of the self?

If we are little worlds, miniature societies, then there must be a parallel between the action of the Spirit of Jesus in the world and the action of the Spirit of Jesus in the heart. What the Spirit struggles to achieve in human societies will throw light on what the Spirit is bringing about in my own conversion and healing. If the Spirit unites people into communities of love where there is room for everyone, then the conversion of each heart will be a similar process of reconciliation. The Spirit will bring the selves of the self into a unity around the center of the indwelling Christ. The New Self will be a kind of inner community based on the principle of love in which there is room for everyone.

Spirit of love, if I am to express the hospitality of God to all sorts of very different people, to people who seem very alien from me, then I need to learn to listen to each one of them very attentively. But how can I pretend to listen carefully to the different people I encounter if I refuse to listen to the different

voices within my own heart? What chance is there of loving and respecting others if I refuse to meet and listen to the many sides of myself? How can I be a reconciler if I shut my ears to the unreconciled conflicts within myself and pretend that I have already arrived at peace?

Now I begin to see that the spiritual life is based on a basic honesty which enables me to recognize that everything I find difficult to accept, bless, forgive, and appreciate in others is actually present within myself. If I paid attention to my own heart I would hear from within many voices, expressing many needs. Perhaps that suspect old saying "charity begins at home" begins to make sense here. Could it be that I have so little charity towards others because I have so little for the many selves of myself?

MEDITATION
Colossians 3:12–15

Friday

EACH OF THE FAITHFUL IS A LITTLE CHURCH

E ach of the faithful is a little church."[5] This is what St. Peter Damian taught his hermits, building on the ancient doctrine that the whole is present in each part. If because I am a person, I am a little world, then because I am a Christian I am becoming a little church. The Spirit in the world takes separate individuals and unites them in Christ, so that they become one body in him:

> For just as the body is one and has many members, and all the members of the body, though many, are one body, so it is with Christ. For in the one Spirit we were all baptized into one body—Jews or Greeks, slaves or free—and we were all made to drink of one Spirit. (1 Corinthians 12:12–13)

Ultimately nothing is to be left outside the fellowship of the Holy Spirit, the new humanity in Christ. God's "plan for the fullness of time [is] to gather up all things in him, things in heaven and things on earth" (Ephesians 1:10). In the same way the Spirit in the heart is seeking to bring each element of our humanity into relationship with the indwelling Christ so that we can become whole. The Spirit reconciles the selves of the self in Christ so that we can embody the unity and peace that is God's will and gift.

The church is only on the way to becoming a true expression of the *koinonia*, the community of the Holy Spirit. In many places it is a travesty, a betrayal, or an only faint approximation of the new community proclaimed in scripture in which "there is no longer Jew or Greek, there is no longer slave or free, there is no longer male and female; for all of you are one in Christ Jesus" (Galatians 3:28). Bur scripture leaves no room for doubt that such a community is what God is forming, and the Spirit reaching from God's future into our present is always striving to bring it about among us. Likewise each one of us is only on the way to being converted into an expression of God's hospitality, a microcosm of the church. The Spirit struggles to bring into unity the disparate persons within us to bring peace.

"Peace," "unity"—these are easy words to fling around. Who is opposed to peace and unity as ideals? But Christ did not emerge from the desert to talk of attractive ideals. He came to actualize the hospitality of God, the new community of God; and the violent opposition he provoked, culminating in his execution on the cross, makes clear that he was striking at the heart of the accepted order in human affairs.

Soon after his testing in the wilderness Jesus preached at his home synagogue in Nazareth.

> He stood up to read, and the scroll of the prophet Isaiah was given to him. He unrolled the scroll and found the place where it was written: "The Spirit of the Lord is upon me, because he has anointed me to bring good news to the poor. He has sent me to proclaim release to the captives and recovery of sight to the blind, to let the oppressed go free, to proclaim the year of the Lord's favor." And he rolled up the

scroll, gave it back to the attendant, and sat down. The eyes of all in the synagogue were fixed on him. Then he began to say to them, "Today this scripture has been fulfilled in your hearing." (Luke 4:16–21)

Jesus proclaims the hospitality of God that beckons all the excluded and disabled and powerless out of the shadows into the full light of day. God's sovereignty is a community in which all have an equal place in the light, a full share of life. At first these words seem welcome to Jesus' neighbors and the synagogue warms with pleasure. But with sickening rapidity it grows cold again. Jesus calmly makes clear that he knows they do not really understand or welcome him. In no time at all the congregation turns into a lynch mob and Jesus narrowly escapes with his life.

The intensity of their resentment is revealing. If the proclamation of the hospitality of God were a benign announcement of religious principles, Jesus would not have provoked the rage of his neighbors. But they realize that Jesus is serving notice that the present arrangements of human society are obsolete. The announcement of God's community of equals requires the abolition of human structures that alienate and oppress and starve out the needy, and that maintain enmities between societies and races. The congregation at Nazareth became enraged because Jesus touched the raw nerve of their contempt for outsiders by pointedly referring to the miracles that Elijah and Elisha did for foreigners. They soon realized that the acceptable year of the Lord threatened to put an end to traditional hostilities. And that they could not tolerate.

The same resistance to the hospitality of God is ingrained in the heart. The Spirit's work in the heart is not a matter of a few adjustments here and there, a little polishing and refining. There has to be a breaking up of the present order. Jesus proclaims to each the acceptable year of the Lord in which all the banished and excluded sides of ourselves can now be welcomed for healing and empowerment. We have been given notice that the false selves we maintain at the cost of excluding so much that is within us are purely provisional arrangements; they must give way to a new way of being. And so the scriptures speak of a breaking down of the old way of being a person and the discovery of a completely new one. They speak of our need to be born again. They speak of crucifying the old self with Christ. Nothing milder than these expressions will do justice to the radical change in our living meant by *metanoia*, the repentance Jesus proclaimed after he emerged from the wilderness.

Jesus is inviting us to participate in his solidarity with humankind, his compassion. But we cannot adopt this compassion as a kind of external pattern of behavior and responses. We have to live that compassion within our own selves. Jesus has to establish the community of reconciliation within the heart. Only by becoming little churches ourselves, societies based on the principle of love in which there is room for everyone, can we take up the "ministry of reconciliation" to which God calls us.

Spirit of Christ, Breath of Christ's Body, I have repented many times, returning to the motherly arms of God, but my lack of compassion shows that a false self still reigns within. There is a way of being myself that has to die before I can live the hospitality of God. You have anointed Christ to release the captives within me and bring about a new community inside me. Help me believe that this day the scripture is being fulfilled.

MEDITATION
1 Corinthians 12 and 13

Saturday

A TREE IS KNOWN
BY ITS FRUIT

By making our own this image of the self as society and grasping the need to be reconciled within ourselves we are responding to one of the most important critiques of conventional Christian spirituality made in this century. Of all the words of Carl Jung, these from his book *Modern Man in Search of a Soul,* written between the wars, have struck home to thinking Christians:

> In actual life it requires the greatest discipline to be simple and the acceptance of oneself is the essence of the moral problem and the epitome of a whole outlook on life. That I feed the hungry, that I forgive an insult, that I love my enemy in the name of Christ—all these are undoubtedly great virtues. What I do unto the least of my brethren, that I do unto Christ. But what if I should discover that the least amongst them all, the poorest of the beggars, the most impudent of all the offenders, the very enemy himself—that these are within me, and that I myself stand in need of the alms of my own kindness—that I myself am the enemy who must be

loved—what then? As a rule the Christian's attitude is then reversed; there is no longer any question of love or long-suffering; we say to the brother
within us "Raca," and condemn and rage against
ourselves. We hide it from the world; we refuse to
admit ever having met this least among the lowly in
ourselves. Had it been God himself who drew near
to us in this despicable form, we should have denied
him a thousand times before a single cock had
crowed.[6]

Jung saw a deep contradiction in much that passed for
Christian morality and spirituality. The acceptance and
forgiveness Christians were encouraged to foster seemed
to be "for export only." Compassion was for others. There
seemed to be hardly any encouragement in conventional
moralistic preaching to be gentle towards one's own pain,
folly, and poverty. So many of the Christians he met were
trying hard to love others while carrying round a burden
of self-rejection. The biblical language of crucifying the old
self had become an instrument of self-punishment instead
of being a metaphor for emancipation from the tyranny of
a false self based on fear. Jung challenged us to be consis-
tent. If Jesus summoned people to have "a single eye," to
find a unity of life and purpose, how could that inner con-
sistency possibly be accomplished if the attitudes they were
to foster towards themselves were the opposites of the ones
they were to adopt with their neighbors—and enemies?

The test of every morality is, of course, "no good tree
bears bad fruit, nor again does a bad tree bear good fruit;
for each tree is known by its own fruit" (Luke 6:43–44).
The deep flaw of inconsistency in the conventional
morality of Christendom was no mere hypothesis of psy-
chologists. It was laid bare in the catastrophic violence of
two world wars and the Holocaust. Christian complicity
and participation in these horrors revealed to us the utter
impossibility of building a world of reconciliation and

peace, while living with war in the heart. "The evil man out of his evil treasure produces evil." In our time the self-hatred and inner dividedness (which conventional Christianity was not only powerless to heal, but actually seemed to cultivate in the name of morality) has boiled over in massive displays of racism and violence. The bitter fruit reveals the nature of the tree. Without an inner climate of compassion in the heart it is not possible to be a peacemaker.

Several months after my discovery of the well I traveled to France to work as a laborer on the building site of the Taizé community, the international, ecumenical brotherhood that has now become one of the great centers for the renewal of Christian life. I remember vividly the impact the community's church made on me when I arrived. Outside the stark and rather unlovely west end of the concrete building was a huge signboard painted in green and yellow. In three languages it repeated the same message, "Be Reconciled!" and listed in columns the relationships in our lives in which reconciliation must be sought. The church was given by Germans in reparation for the war.

As I went on pilgrimage to some of the great medieval churches and cathedrals in Burgundy during my time off from bricklaying, I realized that this uncompromising signboard was the twentieth-century counterpart to the great scenes of the Last Judgment carved over the western doors of so many of them. These depict the dissolving of hierarchical divisions in the presence of the Son of Man on the last day. Crowns and mitres are shown rolling in the dust as men and women were brought naked back to the level of their common humanity. Everyone from grandee to peasant had to pass under this sign on the way in and out of church and submit to this reminder that all divisions of status were only for a time. These awe-inspiring carvings are not easy things to pass under, but neither is the plain signboard at Taizé an easy thing to pass by several times a day. The cathedral carvings at least defer the breakdown of divisions to the last day, whereas the sign at Taizé insists that we face in the here and now the gospel invitation to be reconcilers in a reconciling community, and act upon it. It epitomizes the only authentic spirituality for the twenty-first century, a spirituality and ethos of reconciliation and compassion.

Spirit of God, why have the "Christian nations" been so prone to war? Something must have gone horribly wrong with our way of living the gospel. The quest for a spirituality of reconciliation is something on which the entire credibility of the church now stands or falls. What can I do to play a part in this experiment to recast our spirituality into an instrument of reconciliation? I can at the very least begin with myself and practice upon myself, my selves, the first steps of peacemaking, healing, and compassion. Some of the old ways of understanding the gospel still left self-hatred to do its divisive and destructive work in the heart, and poisoned compassion at the source. If I experiment with a spirituality of acceptance I will be helping with the reconversion of the church.

MEDITATION

Have peace in yourself, and thousands will find salvation around you.

St. Seraphim of Sarov

The Second
Week of Lent

Monday

ALREADY...

There is a truth about ourselves as believers that the Spirit has to make real to us in order for us to cooperate with the inner process of reconciliation. The Spirit needs us to recognize our true center, the actual living core of our persons, the unshakably real self. Unless we come to acknowledge and believe in this true center, we will continue to imagine that our public personalities or our image of ourselves is the whole truth of who we are. We will continue to cling to the self-understanding to which we have become accustomed, and that we sustain by a ceaseless reiteration of our opinions, prejudices, and anxieties. It is too much for most of us to give up the identities we have built up over the years without any sense of what might take their place. That is why we cling even to our hostilities, resentments, and other sins. They are so much a part of us that we cannot imagine what would be left if they were cut away; we doubt that the patient would survive the operation.

The good news of Jesus Christ is that you and I already have a true self. Your real self is already in place. That new self is Jesus Christ living within you.

I have been crucified with Christ; and it is no longer I who live, but it is Christ who lives in me. And the life I now live in the flesh I live by faith in the Son of God, who loved me and gave himself for me. (Galatians 2:19–20)

The work of the Holy Spirit as revealer of truth is the uncovering of this mystery so that we grasp it in faith, or rather so that it grasps us. A new identity, a new being is not dangled in front of our eyes as some elusive goal to which we one day might attain if we struggle hard enough. It is already ours through the undeserved gift of Christ's indwelling. The life of conversion depends on accepting and celebrating this gift so that all the elements within ourselves come into their own round this given center.

The good news is an annunciation. And the annunciation to Mary was not the imparting of information, or the planting of an idea. By the overshadowing of the Holy Spirit she became pregnant! Christ within us by the power of the Spirit is not an idea but a presence even more enfleshed and intimate than a baby in the womb. Jesus, in all the fullness of his ascended glory and in all the living vitality of his undiminished humanity, is fused and united with each one of us.

The conventional Christianity of Christendom took this foundation truth of the gospel and relegated it to the realm of mysticism. Christ in heaven to be obeyed, Christ on earth to be imitated and followed; these themes were kept in conventional teaching. But the baptismal mystery of Christ's union with each believer was allowed to fade almost entirely from consciousness.

Perhaps you have been fortunate and the community of faith to which you belong has nurtured your awareness of "Christ in you, the hope of glory." Be thankful. On the other hand, you may have suffered from the split that has flawed the spirituality of so many churches, in which this vital truth of the gospel has been taken out of circulation and shut away as mysticism for the few.

Either way, this Lent can be an opportunity for the Spirit to help you experience what you already possess in the Christ who is at the heart of your heart. I take the phrase "experiencing what we already possess" from a talk given by Thomas Merton:

> In prayer we discover what we already have through the indwelling Spirit of God and our incorporation through baptism into Christ. You start where you are and deepen what you already have and you real-ize that you are already there. We already have everything but we don't know it and we don't expe-rience it. All we need is to experience what we already possess.[1]

These words perfectly express the Christian experience of grace. Our new selves are given to us without our deserv-ing. We do not make them or achieve them. Our task is to become who we already are.

Merton is assuming a certain understanding of prayer. The prayer he is speaking of is not the performance for God of certain tasks of intercession, thanksgiving, and the like. He speaks of prayer as a means of experiencing what is true. That is what meditation is. In meditation we do not merely think. We let truth take hold of us and experi-ence it. Meditative prayer is receptive. It is an active receptivity in which we allow the Spirit to lead us into truth so that the truth can set us free.

One classic form of meditation lays aside conversation in order to focus on God's presence in the heart in wor-ship, trusting that the Spirit will bring about the changes within myself that we both desire, while I am devoting myself simply to awareness of God. Perhaps the best-known example of this is the practice of the Jesus Prayer, the gentle repetition of the name of Jesus, often framed in a short appeal such as "Lord Jesus Christ, Son of the Living God, have mercy on me, a sinner." In the Jesus Prayer we are letting the presence of God incarnate in the heart become real to us. We are allowing ourselves to identify with him in his compassionate presence within us. We are acknowledging in compunction that we have not yet made his compassion our way of living and being. We are expressing our desire to become more like him. We are expressing both aspects of Paul's words, "I have been crucified with Christ; it is no longer I who live, but it is Christ who lives in me." We experience self-surrender in giving up the preoccupations of our own egos and simply handing over our minds and hearts to the name of Jesus. And in the simple awareness of him we receive a new sense of our true selves as they are in him.

Spirit by whose overshadowing Mary became pregnant with Jesus, Spirit without whom no one can say "Jesus is Lord," your great desire is for me to realize that he is in me, and who I already am in him. Give me the simplicity to believe that the name of Jesus pronounced with love and adoration is more powerful than all my schemes for changing myself for the better. The more I dwell on his indwelling, the more I love him there as he has identified himself with me in utter humility, the more I will become like him. It is by knowing his presence within myself that I will be changed, not by trying to make myself different.

MEDITATION

Now the Lord is the Spirit, and where the Spirit of the Lord is, there is freedom. And all of us, with unveiled faces, seeing the glory of the Lord as though reflected in a mirror, are being transformed into the same image from one degree of glory to another; for this comes from the Lord, the Spirit.

2 Corinthians 3:17–18

Tuesday

ROOTED AND GROUNDED IN LOVE

"Looking our hearts in the face, however difficult that may be" (in the words of the incoherent curate's prayer in Dorothy Sayers's novel) turns out to be even stranger than we thought. If we look with the eyes of faith we see at the center "the glory of God in the face of Jesus Christ" (2 Corinthians 4:6). The face of the Christ who dwells within us is, mysteriously, our own face, our own new identity. Becoming aware of his face at our center makes us realize who we are for the Father, and our prayer begins to find its truest expression in the words of a great hymn, "Look, Father, look on his anointed face, and only look on us as found in him."

But then there are other faces, the faces of the other selves. We are scarcely aware of them; we are reluctant even to acknowledge their existence. The Spirit wants us to experience Christ in relation to them all so that we can discover a new wholeness in ourselves around him. How do we experience Christ interacting with these inner selves?

Think of a story in the Bible that has moved you deeply in the past. Were you moved by a moral derived from the story? Did its power reside in ideas and concepts? That would be unlikely. The scriptures usually have a dramatic impact on us; just as in a great play, we get caught up into the action. The plot mysteriously seems to speak to our condition and to our own struggles, so we find ourselves involved in the scriptural event. Watching a drama, we often half-consciously identify with one of the characters. Meditating on scripture we do the same, so that the challenge issued, the gift given, the answer granted to a certain character becomes ours as well, here and now. The person in the scripture story has symbolized some real aspect of our own selves. By identifying with that person the corresponding personage within ourselves has been raised up and brought into contact with Christ within the realm of awareness. What happens to the person in the story tells us how Christ is now with that aspect of our own selves.

We experience this in hearing the gospels read and preached, in our own Bible reading, and through artworks that depict the stories. And there is a style of meditative prayer that quite deliberately fosters this entrance into the story. In this prayer we allow the Spirit to consecrate our powers of imagination to the full to make the story as vividly alive as possible. We allow ourselves to identify with one of the participants. We pray out of the feelings evoked by experiencing the event from within. We find ourselves able to *be* Zacchaeus, Moses, Mary Magdalene, Jacob, the disciple whom Jesus loved. In each case we experience God in active relationship with some aspect of our own selves that has resonated with the biblical character. This way of praying is so helpful in letting us experience Christ in relationship to the many selves of the heart that I have provided some further guidelines for it at the end of this book.

Now in the following days of this season for the Spirit of truth I am going to invite you to name some aspect of your own total being, such as the child within you, and to allow yourself to experience in meditation something of the way this part of yourself is enfolded in the love of God. In the remaining days only a few persons in your inner community can be brought forward into awareness. In Eastertide and beyond the Spirit can continue the process with fresh encounters. We will return to the same stories and meditations so that the healing work can go deeper each time. The Spirit's work of inner reconciliation will go on as we change and face new challenges as our death grows nearer. In the end the Spirit will recruit the disintegrating power of death to break us up enough to be remade whole once and for all.

Our motive is to grow in the power to love. We want to learn from the Spirit how to "rejoice with those who rejoice, weep with those who weep" (Romans 12:15). This work of prayer is to explore our own reluctance to rejoice and weep over the life within ourselves. Only by keeping company with our own experiences and coming to know how Christ keeps company with us in them will we be able to be "all things to all people" (1 Corinthians 9:22).

I wonder whether a certain irritation has crept into your mind in response to all this talk of love and compassion. Perhaps you find suspicions arising that this is all too introverted, introspective, even sentimental sounding. Do you miss a more robust emphasis on the Lenten call to repentance, strenuous discipleship, conversion? Just take note of these feelings. You can always fling this book away in due course. In time, however, you may discover that confronting within ourselves our deep-dyed negativity, our inveterate tendencies to judge and condemn, our shutting out of what we do not understand, our domination of the weak and fear of the new, is strenuous enough. Adopting the spirituality of compassion is a revolution that casts down the proud and exalts those of low degree.

Come, Holy Spirit! A strange figure of speech indeed. As if you needed to come from or to anywhere, you who fill all things and have been breathed into my being by the Father. You are the one saying "Come" to me! But I need to say to you "Come" in order to express my welcome of your presence and activity. It is my way of saying that I want you to do your work of reconciliation and healing within my heart. You know intimately every part of me. Bring out of the shadows those parts of me that have been put under a ban, or kept out of the light. Let Christ show me what they mean to him and how he is redeeming them.

MEDITATION
Ephesians 3:14–19

Wednesday

ALL THE DYING

W ho forgets the first time he or she witnesses death? I remember reporting to the ward for my first morning at St. Christopher's Hospice in Sydenham not long after it had opened, a rather nervous student hoping to be eased gently into the work. "Will you keep company with Mr... while he dies?" the sister asked me in a matter-of-fact way. For three hours I held the hand of this stranger as he labored over his last breaths. This was a different experience from being with a spouse, a beloved friend, or a member of one's family when we are numb with grief or in anguish at our impending loss. To be with a stranger in this moment of final surrender, without pain of our own getting in the way, is to experience a pure kind of connectedness with another human being. It was a privilege to be permitted to keep company with a dying man. I knew nothing about him except that he had no relatives left. There was no place here for likes and dislikes, knowledge or ignorance. There was only being-with an other following our common destiny. We have compassion on the dying simply as the dying.

A few days later I turned the page of a book I was reading in my hours off and read this:

> Our attitude to all men would be Christian if we
> regarded them as though they were dying, and
> determine our relation to them in the light of death,
> both of their death and our own. A person who is
> dying calls forth a special kind of feeling. Our atti-
> tude to him is at once softened and lifted onto a
> higher plane. We can then feel compassion for peo-
> ple whom we did not love. But every man is dying,
> I too am dying and must never forget about death.[2]

Spiritual life is full of coincidences like this. Nicolas
Berdyaev, the Russian philosopher I was studying, was
interpreting my experience in the hospice ward.

"I too am dying and must never forget about death." In
the old ceremonial of Ash Wednesday the priest dips his
thumb in ashes and makes the sign of the cross on the
foreheads of the worshipers saying, "Remember that you
are dust, and to dust you shall return." The season for the
Spirit of truth begins with the truth we find most difficult
to accept and keep before us, that we are going to die. We
cannot be led by the Spirit into all truth if denial and evasion has gained mastery over us here.

Most human beings flourish on condition that they do
not think of dying. Nursing in a hospice is a good way to
learn the extent to which we collude with one another in
denying our mortality. How much the living want to
deceive the dying by pretending that recovery is round the
corner! What an agony it is for some of the dying themselves to let go of a lifetime's denial and finally acknowledge that their death is approaching! I will never forget
how, while I was giving an old Scotsman with incurable
cancer his bed-bath, I seemed to feel a tremor pass through
his emaciated body, as of inner barriers of avoidance col-
lapsing, when he looked at me and admitted for the first
time that he would be glad when it was all over.

The great spiritual teachers are unanimous in telling us
that freedom depends on our overcoming forgetfulness of

death. We fill our lives with preoccupations in order not to face death. If we become free to look our death in the face in the midst of life then the energies caught up in maintaining these habits and projects can be released for trusting, hoping, and loving.

The Spirit searches and stirs the heart to make me aware that some of the things I fill my life with are my own drugs of choice in humankind's universal game of avoidance of death. The comforts with which I like to cocoon myself, the insistence with which I cling to my fads, opinions, and reputation, the old grievances I nurse, the pastimes with which I soothe the passage of time, the carefulness with which I guard my nest egg or the thrills I get by splashing money around, all these would lose their hold on me if I found the freedom to live fully aware of my mortality and in the tension of hope in the resurrection.

Talking to God often about death, expressing the fear and doubt and awe we feel, can be frightening at first. We are defying a powerful taboo. But the result is not depression. The recollection of death that the Spirit of truth inspires always changes our experience of the present. Now becomes the time to live and to respond. "Therefore, as the Holy Spirit says, 'Today, if you hear his voice, do not harden your hearts'" (Hebrews 3:7). In the state of denial we incessantly postpone reconciling ourselves with people we are estranged from, we put off making new beginnings in our relationships or the way we take care of ourselves, we leave unsaid words of appreciation, love, and gratitude. When those who live in the common state of denial of death are suddenly bereaved then they are haunted by a hundred "if onlys." If only I had made up about this, if only I had told her how much I really loved her. . . .

If in prayer I give a voice to the self who has the courage to break silence about death, it will change my life. Having seen through the games that I played to smother awareness of mortality, I will be able to see through the games others play. I will be more compassionate when I know deep down that beneath the addictions, foibles, and sins of others there is an almost universal fear of death. If I can see through to that inmost secret of others, that they like me are dying, I will be able to tap that compassion for the dying that has been planted deep in the heart.

Spirit of truth, I see now how much my hardness of heart and the way I put off reconciling myself to others and giving them the appreciation and love I know they need is related to my denial of death. The voice of denial constantly whispers that there will always be time to get round to that another day. Your voice speaks of the here and now, and says that as a dying human being among dying brothers and sisters the time to respond with compassion and self-giving is today. How lacking in freedom I am, as long as I carry around this load of unfinished business that accumulates from forgetting death. The truth is that I am not ready to meet others, really meet others, as long as I keep myself unready to die and meet God.

MEDITATION

That brings us to the idea of availability; of being at the disposal of reality and God and truth and people. Asceticism should put a person into a state of freedom where he is ready to die, ready to go forth and meet the Bridegroom at any moment, and there is no unfinished business to fool around with. If we examine ourselves carefully we shall see that most of us have an enormous amount of unfinished business.... We have to be free so that we can just step across the line and that's it. That is what real freedom is.[3]

Thomas Merton

Thursday

NO...AND YES

I f life were simple we could point to those who are neg-ative and closed in upon themselves and say, "Ah, this is because they had a dreadful childhood. Neglect and disappointment must have poisoned their life from the start." And we could assume that those who are open and trusting derived their faith from good parenting and a healthy environment. But life is not simple and the roots of faith not so obvious. Many of those who had a terrible start in life go on to be trusting and risking people. Many of the trapped and lifeless had loving homes.

It appears that almost all of us emerge from childhood equipped with two basic ways of organizing and interpreting our experience of life. However well they are cared for, all babies have frightening experiences of abandonment and helplessness that create an "inner place" where they feel unlovable and from which the world seems hostile and capricious. Conversely, poor parenting has enough patches of health in it to form a tiny, precarious foothold of hope within the child's heart from which the world might look reasonably welcoming, a place where one's needs will be met and some of one's longings realized. So most of us have both places from which to live.

These two standpoints for interpreting life tend to be mutually exclusive. We have all seen ambiguous drawings that can be seen in alternative ways, such as the one that appears either as an elaborate urn or as two faces in profile turned to one another. Human beings tend to interpret life either from the standpoint of mistrust so that life seems full of obstacles and confusion, or from the place of hope so that it seems meaningful and promising. We get stuck in one or another place. Or we oscillate between the two. The nursery rhyme about the little girl with the curl in the middle of her forehead tells us that "when she was good, she was very, very good, and when she was bad, she was horrid."

Jesus confronted people with good news. The word "confront" is important. The good news that we have a God who wants to be called, simply, "Abba," who is in love with creatures, who pours grace into the lives of those prepared to pass it on, confronts and affronts our negation, the No we say to life from the inner standpoint of mistrust. Jesus jolted his hearers out of the perspective of fear into the place of trust.

> But he was in the stern, asleep on the cushion; and they woke him up and said to him, "Teacher, do you not care that we are perishing?" He woke up and rebuked the wind, and said to the sea, "Peace! Be still!" Then the wind ceased, and there was a dead calm. He said to them, "Why are you afraid? Have you still no faith?" (Mark 4:38–40)

Jesus tried to get people to find within themselves that patch of good soil in which he could plant the little seed of Yes to God that could grow into a great tree.

> Have faith in God. Truly I tell you, if you say to this mountain, "Be taken up and thrown into the sea," and if you do not doubt in your heart, but believe that what you say will come to pass, it will be done

for you. So I tell you, whatever you ask for in prayer, believe that you have received it, and it will be yours. (Mark 11:22–24)

Jesus' passionate summons to men and women to say Yes with him to a loving God at work in the real world is risky. The danger is that we may hear it as an invitation to naive optimism, reliance on the "amazing power of positive thinking" beloved of the breezy American merchants of religious uplift. But what makes Jesus' invitation to faith different is that he prevents his hearers from repressing in the name of faith all the hard evidence in life that counts against hope. The faith he lived and was releasing into the world was a faith that said Yes while steadily looking into the face of everything that seems to make No the right answer to life in a harsh world. He spoke of persecution and poverty, of desertion and death. And in the end it was not a matter of speaking at all. In Jesus' abandonment and execution, in his cry of desolation from a cross that put him under the curse of the holy law, in "the darkness over the whole earth until the ninth hour," God allowed the evidence of his seeming absence and powerlessness to come forth with all its savage power to rip our trust to shreds.

It is only after this devastating exposure of all that counts on the side of No that God pronounced the decisive Yes by raising Jesus from the dead on the third day.

The Spirit can help me today to understand a little better the interplay of Yes and No in my life. There is a self within me that says No to hope, No to myself, No to others, No to opportunities, the self that allows everything to take on the darkness and rigidity of that cave inside where life seems frustrating and hurtful. Can I be aware of this self with compassion? Can I see within myself the same place where so many of my fellow human beings are trapped, their lives so resigned, so stiff with quiet desperation?

Can I also hear within myself the voice that pronounces a real Yes to God and to the life in which I meet God? The Spirit can tune my awareness to distinguish this Yes from the Yes of naiveté that whistles a happy tune to hold at bay the menace of life's dangers and sufferings. Can I hear within myself a voice that says Yes back to the Yes of God who raised Jesus—the one who had been handed over to death and failure? Can I hear a Yes from within that trusts and believes, that hopes and asks, that reaches and strives, that accepts and receives? Can I hear within myself a Yes that trusts the love of God, and accepts our extreme vulnerability at the same time without pretense? Can I hear a Yes from within myself that is deep because it is an acceptance of a way of love that works *through* our vulnerability?

Breath of God in me, God has said Yes to me by giving you to me as my helper and source of the new life I want. The faith you are giving me will help my Yes to life gradually to sound stronger than the No of my mistrust. The hope you are stirring in me will help my Yes overcome my timidity. The love with which you are impregnating me will melt the barriers behind which I have been taught to live and help me say Yes to myself, to others, and to the God in whom we all live and move and have our being.

MEDITATION

You dare your Yes—and experience a meaning. You repeat your Yes—and all things acquire a meaning. When everything has a meaning, how can you live anything but a Yes. [4]

Dag Hammarskjöld

As surely as God is faithful, our word to you has not been "Yes and No." For the Son of God, Jesus Christ, whom we proclaimed among you, Silvanus and Timothy and I, was not "Yes and No"; but in him it is always "Yes." For in him every one of God's promises is a "Yes." For this reason it is through him that we say the "Amen," to the glory of God. But it is God who establishes us with you in Christ and has annointed us by putting his seal on us and giving us his Spirit in our hearts as a first installment.

2 Corinthians 1:18–22

Friday

EVERYONE ENTERS THE KINGDOM OF GOD VIOLENTLY . . . ?

From the days of John the Baptist until now the kingdom of heaven has suffered violence, and the violent take it by force. (Matthew 11:12)

This saying of Jesus recorded by Matthew puzzles interpreters and there is no agreement about what precisely he is referring to in "the Jesus movement" in Palestine. But the saying does not appear to deplore the force with which some people are breaking into the realm of God's hospitality and grace. The version of the same saying used by Luke implied that this force is something *everybody* needs in order to enter the kingdom. "The law and the prophets were in effect until John came; since then the good news of the kingdom of God is proclaimed, and everyone tries to enter it by force" (Luke 16:16).

One of the endlessly fascinating features of the composite image of Jesus built up by the gospels is that he was a man of gentleness *and* force. In the very next chapter Matthew can apply to Jesus Isaiah's words about the

Suffering Servant, "He will not break a bruised reed or quench a smoldering wick" (Matthew 12:20). There is no sense of inconsistency between Jesus declaring that he is meek and lowly of heart, and his violent overturning of the tables of the moneychangers and animal-sellers in the temple, his blessing of the little children and his blistering denunciation of the religious authorities. If we are really to know Jesus present in our own hearts, "the same yesterday and today and for ever," we had better be prepared for both tenderness and anger.

If the thought of facing Jesus' anger is troubling and repellent, that is probably a sign that we have trouble in giving a place to "the forceful one" in our own inner society. What do we do with our aggression? Where is our anger? If we are not prepared to face our own aggression and bring it into contact with the forcefulness of Jesus, then this element of our humanity will be left unredeemed. Unredeemed, it will poison our lives and through us the lives of our neighbors.

How did Jesus demonstrate that aggression can be holy? He showed that aggression can provide the energy for us to assert the primacy of love, to cut away all that is not love, to differentiate the important from the trivial, to provide the strength to separate the authentic from the false and pretentious. When Jesus challenged the mourning man to "leave the dead to bury their own dead," when he cursed the fig tree and denounced the Pharisees, this is what he was doing. Jesus could not be holy without using his anger. Nor can we.

What do we do with our anger? Often we are so afraid of it that we deny and suppress it behind false smiles. So it smoulders below like a fire deep down in a ship's hold, with the fumes seeping out here and there, igniting now and then in nasty remarks and peevish moods. Or anger rejected and bottled up inside leaks out and eats away at our own self-esteem like a caustic, inducing depression. We endow others with our own unlived aggression. We become terribly hurt by others' remarks because we inflate their anger with our own, which we are refusing to acknowledge and use. Or we allow anger, still disconnected from the love of God poured into our hearts, to grab the reins and drive us in this direction and that, trampling others down on the way. Religious people driven about by unhallowed aggression must often justify themselves by giving the name "righteous indignation" to these excursions. The correspondence columns of ecclesiastical newspapers show how nasty are the results of trying to counterfeit holy wrath. The list of what unredeemed anger does to us is endless. This is where the wounds of human fallenness are most deep.

We must love our capacity to be forceful, love our aggression, as God loved and loves it in Jesus. First, it means honestly expressing in prayer what actually does arouse our anger, including the way God seems to treat us. Only when we vent and name our anger can we be open to the purification, healing, and redirection of our anger. This is a humiliating and messy business, because it compels us to recognize two things. First, how much energy we expend smothering the rage caused by past injuries, pretending that "it was nothing, really..." and that we have no need of the healing and consolation of God. Second, the extent to which we pervert and trivialize the God-given energy of aggression. We fret and fume over minute frustrations, but as for the outrageous injustices in the world, in the church, and in our own local communities that cry out before God for correction, we feel almost nothing beyond a vague sense that "there's nothing I can do about it." A passionate God tries to stimulate and recruit our passion, and we resist by numbing and dissipating it. The absurdity is that we think we are being penitent as we confess to God in our prayers that we have been angry, when our real sin is our dogged refusal to let the Spirit arouse our anger in the causes of love and justice.

In Christian spirituality, whether of the early western monks or the Puritans of New England, the story of Jacob wrestling with the angel has had enormous importance. This story is about you. You will never go forward, never be blessed unless you are prepared to struggle with God and let God's arms get round the violence that is in you.

❧

Holy fire, everyone enters the kingdom of God violently. No one can become a peacemaker if she or he tries to leave aggression outside. We have to bring our aggression into our intimacy with God so it can keep on being healed and redirected. I would dearly like to avoid this discipline if I could. This is where you are stern with me. The anger that is part of me seems intrinsically unlovable and dangerous. Maybe it can become holy in the saints and prophets, but not in me.

You are the Spirit of the God of Jacob, you are the Spirit of Jesus who called himself "the strong man, fully armed," devoted to getting us out of prison. Letting Jesus evoke and convert the forceful woman, the strong man, in me will be the work of years not a day, but today I can start again in a small way. How do you want me to pray my anger now?

MEDITATION

The same night he got up and took his two wives, his two maids, and his eleven children, and crossed the ford of the Jabbok. He took them and sent them across the stream, and likewise everything that he had. Jacob was left alone; and a man wrestled with him until daybreak. When the man saw that he did not prevail against Jacob, he struck him on the hip socket; and Jacob's hip was put out of joint as he wrestled with him. Then he said, "Let me go, for the day is breaking." But Jacob said, "I will not let you go, unless you bless me." So he said to him, "What is your name?" And he said, "Jacob." Then the man said, "You shall no longer be called Jacob, but Israel, for you have striven with God and with humans, and have prevailed." Then Jacob asked him, "Please tell me your name." But he said, "Why is it that you ask my name?" And there he blessed him. So Jacob called the place Peniel, saying, "For I have seen God face to face, and yet my life is preserved." The sun rose upon him as he passed Penuel, limping because of his hip.

Genesis 32:22–31

Saturday

BODY

Thank God our preoccupations do not succeed in monopolizing our attention all the time, so occasionally we find ourselves looking up and around, and being taken off guard by the beauty of creation, the wonder of it. We gaze at the stars or the water or the hills, and awe brings us close to God for a moment. As I write I can look through the window across a frozen beach to the tip of Cape Cod; seals are playing in the water in the dazzling brightness of the low winter sun.

The danger is that occasional moments like these can lull us into thinking that we are already good enough lovers of God's creation, when the truth is we have hardly even begun to guess what that means. The heart of any fool can rise to a scene like the midwinter transfiguration spread out before me, but only a heart converted to mercy, in St. Isaac's words, "burns for all creation, for men and birds and animals and demons and for every creature." A painful test of truth for many is when the Spirit calls us from looking at lovely scenery back to our own bodies—now what of this creation of God? Where is our love for this?

Teilhard de Chardin once wrote that "my matter," my body, is not a bit of the universe that I possess totally. It is the whole of the universe possessed by me partially. This strange thought is the modern equivalent of the ancient doctrine of the human person as microcosm, the world in miniature. Love for matter, for the cosmos of God's making, like charity, begins at home. How can I love God's creation if I fail to love that world as it exists summed up in my own body?

When an acquaintance loves someone we do not find attractive we sometimes express puzzlement in the form of the question: "What does she see in him?" If we asked God, "What do you see in me, in my body?" the answers might amaze us indeed.

God sees in our bodies the sum of countless acts of creation and transformation over aeons of cosmic time. Origen said that we have within us the sun and the moon and also the stars. It is literally true. For instance, every carbon atom in our bodies was formed in a star when three helium nuclei collided in one spot within less than a millionth of a millionth of a second. We are children of the stars. Every constituent of our bodies has had a million other lives in the seas, in plants, in animals. In every cell and organ God reads the history of our evolution over millennia and the links by which we are connected with the entire network of living beings. And God sees everything that he has made epitomized and summed up in our bodies—and behold, it is very good.

God sees in our bodies the limbs and organs of the Body of Christ. The Word became flesh, and when we are baptized into Christ our flesh is incorporated into his Body, becoming in him a further extension of divine indwelling and transformation. "Do you not know that your bodies are members of Christ?" (1 Corinthians 6:15). So in our bodies God sees not just creation, but creation being reconciled and transfigured. Therefore God sees in our bodies not only the past but the future of all creation. Our bodies—the concrete reality of our unique lives, our acts and passions, our relationships, memories, and achievements—are destined to be taken up into the divine life as part of the final integration of all things through Christ.

The Spirit yearns for us to know what God sees in us. But for us to accept it means the unlearning of ingrained negativity about the body. Many of us soaked up in our childhoods a lot of shame about our bodies. The education we received developed the intellect but often did little to cultivate our senses or intensify our awareness of beauty or foster our sense of intimacy with nature. The supposedly Christian spirituality handed on to us was eloquent about restraint and morality and tended to deepen rather than heal our suspicion that the senses, our bodies, and sexuality were essentially enemy territory for God. The secular ethos of consumerism that encourages our gratification of every sense offers no healing either. It leaves untouched the cold core of self-hatred that masses of people carry in their bodies.

The cultures that gave us this disincarnate and moralistic spirituality and its perverse twin of exploitative consumerism have laid the earth open to pollution and ruin. Since we are on the way to destroying the earth, discovering a spirituality of love for the earth, a spirituality of embodiment and connectedness with nature is so far from being a fad for would-be mystics that it is essential for saving the planet. How I feel about my body, how I come to my senses in order to know my connectedness with the earth and the web of life, is a crucial matter. I can either experience in myself the healing and repentance that is needed on a massive scale to save the earth, or inertia can condemn me to remain part of the problem of alienation instead of part of its solution.

Exploring through prayer the truth about my attitude to my body, and Christ's attitude towards it as the place where he lives, is a vulnerable business. It includes the healing of memories where I learned, perhaps through ridicule, to despise some elements of my appearance. It needs to experiment, perhaps by praying naked, to bring to Christ the embarrassment which reveals that I lack confidence and happiness in my own embodiment and need to ask God to give me that. It examines the way I fail to use my body and powers of touch to bless and help others through tenderness. It risks venturing into precarious areas, like my fear of physical sickness and death. It tests in the presence of God how genuine is my acceptance of my womanhood or manhood and my thankfulness for it. It opens me to judgment as the Spirit shows me any tendencies to neglect and abuse my body. It turns me outward to the world, and gets me to ask for grace day by day to delight in my senses and use them to stay alert, connected, and appreciative.

Spirit of love, teacher of love, let me learn from you love of my own body. How many times have I approached the altar and fed on the body and blood of Christ without realizing what this means, that my body is being more deeply integrated into him, and is truly holy? Spirit of fire, I want you to burn away within me any useless shame that lurks there, my blindness to the

glory of creation, my indifference to the needs of creatures and the threats that menace this fragile earth, our home.

MEDITATION

The Jews then disputed among themselves, saying, "How can this man give us his flesh to eat?" So Jesus said to them, "Very truly, I tell you, unless you eat the flesh of the Son of Man and drink his blood, you have no life in you. Those who eat my flesh and drink my blood have eternal life, and I will raise them up on the last day; for my flesh is true food and my blood is true drink. Those who eat my flesh and drink my blood abide in me, and I in them. Just as the living Father sent me, and I live because of the Father, so whoever eats me will live because of me.

John 6:52–57

The Third
Week of Lent

Monday

HONOR YOUR FATHER AND YOUR MOTHER

There is a point in the short story *A Set of Variations on a Common Theme* by Frank O'Connor, one of modern Ireland's great writers, where we are brought to the edge of a deep issue in our relationships with our parents. Kate Mahoney is a widow who fosters unwanted illegitimate children. She cannot bring herself to tell Jimmy that he is not her son, but one night he guesses and she has to tell him that "Aunt Nance" is his real mother:

> He said nothing for a while, then he asked in a low voice, "And who was my daddy?"
>
> "How would I know who he was? Whoever he was, he wasn't much."
>
> "When I find out I'm going to kill him."
>
> "Indeed you'll do nothing of the sort," she said sharply. "Whatever he did, he is your father and you wouldn't be here without him. He's there inside you, and the thing you will slight in yourself will be the rock you will perish on."[1]

There is a truth about our relationship with our parents which can only be approached by making the strange assertion, "They are there inside us." Unless we can love them "there," our taking care of them may be not much more than the performance of a duty. Unless we can love them there, some part of ourselves will be starved and slighted.

They are there because they endowed us with their genes. Studies of identical twins separated at birth and then reunited and compared as adults reveal that as much as half of our behavior patterns and preferences are inherited from our parents and forebears. They are there in our bodies that reproduce the features they had inherited. They are there because their care-giving and raising of us have shaped us. They are there as a complex of impressions and memories shot through with love and pain, and charged with the alternating current of our acceptance of their authority and our reaction against it.

How does Christ at the heart of our hearts weave his love into all this? The first way he does it hardly looks like love at all. Christ summons us to freedom through detachment from our parents. We might prefer the gospels to have recorded a lot of teaching inculcating perpetual devotion to parents and family, but instead they present us with the shock treatment of sayings like, "I have come to set a man against his father, and a daughter against her mother. . . . Whoever loves father or mother more than me is not worthy of me" (Matthew 10:35, 37). A certain freedom from their parents comes to most people through marriage, but the freedom Christ is speaking of goes much farther than that. Entering the sovereignty of God is an act that revolutionizes life. Through it we realize that the authority children see invested in their parents and adults rightly belongs to the God who is all. In conversion we restore it to our one-and-only Father, who is revealed in Jesus as self-giving love, allowing to others only that reduced and relative authority that is compatible with the absolute claims of God.

Simple as it sounds, the discovery that only God is God is the greatest one we will ever make. Much evil in life stems from regarding as divine what is, and was meant to be, only human. When we learn to "call no man father on earth because you have only one Father and he is in heaven," we can let our parents be the fallible, limited human beings they really are. Were they tender and caring? Thank God. Were they crazy and cruel? Then if we let Christ take back the divinity with which our infant selves endowed them, we can start dealing with the pain they inflicted on us (as no doubt it had been inflicted on them). We can seek patiently the supernatural grace to forgive even extreme abuse and discover how much misdirected resentment against God inevitably festered in our unhealed wounds.

It is intensely important for God that we come to honor aright those who bore and raised us. If we are stuck with resentment against them, that resentment can block awareness of God's mothering/fathering love. If we remain bound up with them we will expect of them what only God can provide. If we despise them the scorn will rebound on ourselves, since so much of us is from them. Furthermore, alienation from our parents will mar the quality of our action for God as fellow-workers with the Holy Spirit in building inclusive communities. Sometimes in the behavior of those who are filled with reforming zeal for church and society there is evidence of such a failure of acceptance, as if their program of getting people to change is a way of acting out a hidden need to correct and even punish their parents.

"He is our peace." As Christ seeks to embrace us and our parents within his peace he would have us bear in mind his own human struggle. The gospels, which might have so idealized his relations with his parents, reveal that truth and peace are costly and that there is necessarily pain in the journey from dependence to independence and through independence to the maturity out of which we can honor our parents. The boy Jesus stays behind in the temple without much regard for his parents' feelings. His mother and his brothers come to get him when his ministry passes beyond the bounds of what they can understand. Jesus challenges Mary at Cana about her right to intervene. A sword passes through Mary's heart in her relationship with her Son, as Simeon foretold. Christ knows there is nothing simple about the relations between parents and offspring.

Spirit of God, the truth we need to wrestle with in order to fulfill the commandment to honor father and mother has so many aspects! There is nothing easy here. You are the Creator Spirit. You want me to recognize that my parents were your instruments in making me the utterly unique being that I am. Help me love what they gave me and made of me, and honor my own self which, through them, you made to be a member of Christ's Body.

You are the Spirit of truth and love. Help me shed the illusions that prevent me from seeing them as they really were and are, and the conditions I impose on my love for them.

MEDITATION

Read 1 Corinthians 13 with your parents in mind. What is there in this kind of love that they were able to give you? What aspect of the love described here were they not able to give you? What is there about this God-given love that you particularly need to pray for in order to truly honor them in your heart?

Tuesday

THE ONE WHO DESIRES

The Spirit and the bride say, "Come." And let everyone who hears say, "Come." And let everyone who is thirsty come. Let anyone who wishes take the water of life as a gift. (Revelation 22:17)

These are almost the last words of scripture, an invitation to men and women of desire.

Would you identify yourself as one who desires? If that is hardly how you usually think of yourself, you are far from alone. Words like "desire," "passion," and "ecstasy" have come to have associations of sexuality, and we have received little encouragement, to say the least, to be sexual beings in the presence of God. It is as though the woman or man of passion within ourselves has been banished from the presence of God, except when expressly summoned for the purposes of confessing transgressions. Few people pray easily about their sexuality or readily let go in their love of God with the abandon of the psalmist who sang, "O God, you are my God, I seek you, my soul thirsts for you; my flesh faints for you" (Psalm 63:1).

There is something shameful about the eagerness many Christians show in railing against the so-called abandonment of Christian standards with regard to sex. If the erotic has been so profaned, we have contributed greatly to that profanation by cutting it off from its roots in the holy. Those who know little of the living God still long, as humans must, for transcendence, ecstasy, passion; in our technological society sex is the last place where there seems to be a chance of finding it. Dare we blame them for not finding much promise of ecstasy in the colorless, dehydrated religion of so many churches?

What would it involve if we were to experience God's hallowing embrace of the passionate and erotic self? A first step is to defy the taboo against expressing to God in prayer our current feelings about our sexuality. For some that might mean sharing with God memories or current experience of sexual fulfillment and childbearing in a spirit of thankfulness. For others it might mean summoning the courage to ask for love to come into their lives. Others will be taken into a painful area where they must share with God emptiness and frustration and the disappointment of their hopes. There are prayers of honesty that acknowledge that sexuality seems to have been relatively unimportant in life, and others that say how much, very much, it matters. There are prayers of confusion and mixed feelings about wanting sex outside the limits set by the wisdom of God in the covenant. There are the distinctive prayers of homosexual men and lesbian women who struggle for integrity as they long to express intimacy in ways that have been banned by church and society.

Only when we bring into the light of prayer the many feelings we have about our sexuality can we begin to experience the healing of the split between sex and the sacred that has harmed us so profoundly. But this is only the beginning, We need to reach a level of self-awareness at which we know that, whatever our experience of sexual union is or is not, there is at our center a deep need to be desired, and a deep need to desire. The sacredness of the erotic in ourselves consists in the holiness and validity of this twofold need. Sexual union is the clue woven into the very fibers of our being of the promised union between ourselves and the God of love. You are found infinitely desirable by God. You will find God infinitely desirable, the One who, unlike our fellow-creatures, can be loved without reserve or limit, with all the brakes off.

It is puzzling for modern Christians to discover that our believing ancestors seem to have had a much deeper sense that to love God with all our heart, and with all our mind, and with all our soul, and with all our strength means we must draw from the deepest wellspring of erotic energy within us. How astonishing that by the end of the Middle Ages the Song of Songs had more commentaries written on it than any other book of the Bible, over two hundred and forty! "Happy is the one who has no less a desire for God than that of a lover crazy about his beloved," proclaimed St. John of the Ladder to his monks on Mount Sinai.

In prayer, in our relationship with God, we can experiment with using new language that has deeper roots in our sexuality. Perhaps if we prayed about being in love with God our relationship with the Holy One might begin to shed its formality and stiffness and we could begin to enter into the experience of the intimacy God has already established with us in Christ. If the woman or man of desire within us had more opportunity to speak the language of desire and adoration and self-yielding we would find ourselves able to break through our projections of God as taskmaster to discover God as Absolute Beauty. We would discover that the power God has over us is the power to attract us with the utter beauty of Holiness. Because few people around us seem willing to tell us of the beauty of God, the tenderness of God, the desire of God for us, we have to learn of these things ourselves by taking risks in our praying. Almost the only help we can get is from the mystics of the church, who discovered long ago that the truth at the heart of all truth is that God is in love with us, and that every single human being is made by God to be a great lover.

The more we can begin to find the blessing of the erotic in us, as we become in the fullest meaning of the word *lovers* of God, the more we will be able to be compassionate with our brothers and sisters who flounder, hurt people, suffer and lose themselves in sex and love. We will not want to throw the first stone, knowing how hurt and confused and vulnerable we all are in our sexuality and lives of intimacy and how impossible it is for this element in our lives to come right until we have experienced the total acceptance of the Holy One.

Spirit of God, living in the depths of my being, you live and move at the very source of my sexuality and energy of desire. Unless you keep on rekindling my life at its source my faith can become dry and dutiful. God can seem remote and severe. My heart can become dull and resigned. At Pentecost you came as flame. "Come down, O Love divine, seek thou this soul of mine and kindle it, thy holy flame bestowing," so that I can awake to the reality of God's desire for me, and mine for God.

MEDITATION

But now thus says the LORD, he who created you, O Jacob, he who formed you, O Israel: Do not fear, for I have redeemed you; I have called you by name, you are mine. When you pass through the waters, I will be with you; and through the rivers, they shall not overwhelm you; when you walk through fire you shall not be burned, and the flame shall not consume you. For I am the LORD your God, the Holy One of Israel, your Savior. I give Egypt as your ransom, Ethiopia and Seba in exchange for you. Because you are precious in my sight, and honored, and I love you, I give people in return for you, nations in exchange for your life.

Isaiah 43:1–4

Read the Song of Solomon. Cherish words of tenderness in it as words of God to you, and of you to God.

Wednesday

THE WOUNDED CHILD

Truly, I tell you, unless you change and become like children, you will never enter the kingdom of heaven. (Matthew 18:3)

It is hard for us to grasp how to do this turning. We cannot become like children by an external mimicry. Any such idea is entirely adult in conception; the project of becoming like a child is self-contradictory. It is no use looking at children and trying to figure out what to copy. We have to meet the child within us and let Christ bring her or him to life.

The stained-glass windows and "children's corner" pictures that disfigure so many churches with a mawkish Jesus patting cute infants of various races are a travesty of the gospel accounts of Jesus' contact with children. These portray an unsentimental man fiercely aware of the vulnerability of children to abuse by adults. After Jesus' warning that it is essential that we turn and become like children, Matthew continues with chilling words about how some children are damaged by the unspeakable cruelty of adults.

> Whoever welcomes one such child in my name welcomes me. If any of you put a stumbling block before one of these little ones who believe in me, it would be better for you if a great millstone were fastened around your neck and you were drowned in the depth of the sea. (18:5–6)

Stained-glass windows may portray Jesus taking children in his arms and blessing them, but I have never seen one depicting Jesus a moment or two before, enraged with his disciples for preventing people from bringing their children to him. The story is not only about the tenderness of Jesus and his delight in children; it is as much about his grief and anger over the ways adults can block and suppress them.

We are unlikely to be able to become like little children if we deny their suffering. Those of us who know many adults who were subjected to incest and sexual abuse as children and have been initiated into the facts about how the phenomenon is not a rare crime confined to dens of iniquity, but is woven into the texture of family life in all our neighborhoods, also know how resistant most people are to facing these facts. And crimes of emotional and physical violence against children are not inexplicable horrors completely unrelated to the way "good" parents bring them up, but rather extreme examples of the tendency to resort to force with children—a tendency that lurks in the hearts of all of us. I suspect Simon Bar-Jonah was a wonderful father, but he had no qualms about forcing the little children away from Jesus when they were brought to him.

Scripture speaks of the "mystery of iniquity." We cannot understand evil, since it is intrinsically absurd, but we are bound to look into the mystery and not let its obscurity be our pretext for looking away. If we as Christians hold the doctrine of original sin, we must look into that. A friend of mine who has devoted twenty years, day in day out, to giving psychotherapy to perpetrators of incest and sexual abuse tells me that in every case she has ever dealt with the abusers had themselves been abused as children. This helps me look into one aspect of the mystery of iniquity. At birth we enter into a fateful cycle of repetition. Wounded slightly or seriously in the early years of our development, the patterns of force to which we were subjected tug at us in our adult lives from below as a psychological undertow, influencing us to repeat them on our own children.

Breaking the cycle is like being born again and it cannot be done without letting the love of God surround our own woundedness with nurture and healing. When Jesus stopped his teaching session and spent the rest of the time caressing and blessing the children who were brought to him, he was demonstrating something essential for the *adults* he had confronted and who were now watching him. They needed to turn and become as little children who are not ashamed of their desire and need to be held.

It is precisely this repressive adult shame that deters so many people from the practice of prayer, because in prayer we are not just conducting "serious adult business" with the ruler of life. We are allowing ourselves to be folded into the arms of the all-embracing one whom Jesus called "Abba," and whom the psalmist refers to in this image:

> I do not occupy myself with great matters, or with things that are too hard for me. But I still my soul, and make it quiet like a child upon its mother's

breast; my soul is quieted within me. (Psalm
131:2–3)

I have invited many people to identify themselves in
meditation with someone or other taking part in the inci-
dent in which Jesus took the children into his arms, and
their accounts have always moved me. Some of them have
experienced the story as the disciples, and in the presence
of Christ have faced that repressive side of themselves that
keeps the inner child down. A few have experienced it
through Christ's eyes and have felt his anger against the
exclusion of children and his delight in them. Most have
chosen to experience the whole thing from knee height, as
it were, as one of the children, and have found themselves
not only in touch with their own bewilderment at being
forced this way and that by contending adults, but also a
deep satisfaction in being taken in Jesus' arms. Letting go
of their adult accusations of sentimentality has enabled
them to realize a continuing need to be cared about, held,
touched, and blessed without reference to achievements.
They have allowed the child within them to enter into
her or his rightful place close to the Christ within them.

*Holy Spirit, you are the secret of Jesus' passion against the
forces that wound and shrivel the lives of the young and you are
the source of his love for them. You are the only one who can
enable us to turn and become like children in response to that
love. Take away from me my fear of a child's vulnerability.
Help me recognize that I am also a wounded child; otherwise I
may bar myself from the kingdom. Only by risking that vulnerability can I lay myself open to the limitless love of the one
whom I then shall be truly calling "Abba, Father."*

MEDITATION

The cry to God as Father in the New Testament is not a calm acknowledgment of a universal truth about God's abstract "fatherhood," it is the child's cry out of nightmare.[2]

Rowan Williams

People were bringing little children to him in order that he might touch them; and the disciples spoke sternly to them. But when Jesus saw this, he was indignant and said to them, "Let the little children come to me; do not stop them; for it is to such as these that the kingdom of God belongs. Truly I tell you, whoever does not receive the kingdom of God as a little child will never enter it." And he took them up in his arms, laid his hands on them, and blessed them.

Mark 10:13–16

Thursday

THE CHILD
OF GLORY

The soul is as young as it was when it was created. Old age concerns only the soul's use of the bodily senses. . . . My soul is as young as it was when it was created. Yes, and much younger! I tell you it would not surprise me if it were younger tomorrow than it is today![3]

We can almost see Meister Eckhart's eyes twinkling as he preaches. But this is not paradox for the sake of effect. He means it. The mystics get beyond the imagery of God as the Ancient of Days, which has such a hold on the imaginations of believers and unbelievers alike, and experience "God all bounteous, all creative" as the inexhaustibly fresh, the ever-resplendently new source of all newness from whom all being continually pours. God is the *novissimus*, the newest of all. The closer we get to God, the more God can bestow on us a share of that inexhaustible newness which we call eternity.

Sometimes in the last hours of holy people their faces shine with an uncanny youthfulness. But that is only a special manifestation of what we constantly observe in the lives of old men and women who are friends of God. They have a playfulness, an openness, a spontaneity, a trust, an undimmed eye for the beauty of creation which shows that, enlivened by the Spirit, they have allowed themselves to become younger. Conversely, there are vast numbers of young people who have already made their pact with death and grown old in sterility and boredom.

We could say that there is within our inner community not only a wounded child, but a child of glory. That child is the self through whom we have access to the vitality and youthfulness of God. She or he is the one who reflects the creativity, sensitivity, and vibrant imagination of the Love who is our maker and mother. The enemy of human nature wants to destroy this child of glory within us, just as Herod wanted to destroy Mary's child, whose birth threatened his regime. There can be a massacre of the innocents in the heart; there has to be whenever the powers that be there choose the way of greed, senseless hedonism, mediocre agnosticism, or deadly serious religion.

"I came that they may have life, and have it abundantly" (John 10:10). Jesus' mission was to inaugurate a life-giving community of the enlivened. He used to take children and set them before the disciples and insist that they be taken as models of leadership. Children have *authority* in the kingdom; they embody and communicate the vulnerability, the openness, the *élan*, the reaching-out-for-life of God's Spirit.

Where the authority of the child is denied there will inevitably be spiritual sickness. One of the things God is doing with the church today, as it is purged and humiliated by the fading of its prestige and its loss of power, is exposing its long-standing sins to the light. Hundreds of churches dare not claim that they represent the abundance of life Jesus came to bring, or manifest the fire he came to cast upon the earth. Plain for all to see is worship leaden with deadly seriousness or hollow with triviality, relationships petty and self-concerned, an ethos flat with boredom. In the churches where the child has been stifled, there seems no air left to breathe—or else it is rank with the acrimony of ecclesiastical controversy.

The repentance of the church begins with my repentance. The Spirit who is the Lord and Giver of Life is calling me to examine how much authority I allow to the child of glory within me.

The authority of the child is the authority of the future. The Spirit comes from God's future into our present in order to open up our present to becoming that future. The Spirit does not come to us in a pipeline from the past but blows upon us from the future. The spirit is the God "who is to come." I recognize the authority of the child when I stop insisting on what I am and loosen my grip on what I have been, when I continually open myself in prayer to what God is inviting me to become and recognize that I can be born again and again and again. I am still malleable, new buds appear, new gifts can be bestowed. My mind can change, my horizons open up. I am like a child: educable and in formation, and again and again in prayer I praise God in the words, "So if anyone is in Christ, there is a new creation: everything old has passed away; see, everything has become new!" (2 Corinthians 5:17).

The authority of the child is the primacy of imagination and play. I recognize that authority when I allow myself to have fun, to let go, to let the air out of my own adult pomposity. I admit new gusts of the Spirit through fresh appreciation of the arts that rekindle my imagination and prepare me to be stimulated again into life by the imagery of the scriptures and the liturgy. I love that child and welcome its power by permitting myself to dream and to feel.

The authority of the child is the importance of wonder. Creation is wonderful, the Creator is glorious. Without the wonder I cannot enjoy the glory through praise. I must repent by stripping from my perceptions the film of familiarity that causes me to be bored (sacrilege!) beneath the shining skies. I must implore the Spirit to open my child's inner eye to see the mystery and beauty and intense significance of the ordinary things of life. Only through that will I be able to see the glory and greatness of the Creator. Our alienated adulthood is so powerful that I must do this again and again.

⁂

Lord and giver of life, you bring to mind the words of Jesus, "Whoever receives one such child in my name receives me." Receiving the child within me is one of the ways I receive him into my life.

And vice versa. Receiving the Christ child in prayer helps me welcome myself as a child of glory. It is not good for me to think of Jesus as an infant merely for a few days around Christmas. I must contemplate often the Child of God dwelling in this stable which my heart is, and let my love for him in his defenselessness and humility overflow as love for the child who I am. How much cynicism, boredom, and calculation sullies my life! How easy it is to become estranged from the child of glory!

MEDITATION
John 3:1–10

Then they came to Capernaum; and when he was in the house he asked them, "What were you arguing about on the way?" But they were silent, for on the way that had argued with one another who was the greatest. He sat down, called the twelve, and said to them, "Whoever wants to be first must be last of all and servant of all." Then he took a little child and put it among them; and taking it in his arms, he said to them, "Whoever welcomes one such child in my name welcomes me, and whoever welcomes me welcomes not me but the one who sent me."

Mark 9:33–37

Friday

THE REPEAT OFFENDER

"I want to drive sin out of my life," says the Christian. "That's right," says Pride, "and I am going to help you. That way things will be peaceful for both of us."[4]

The French novelist Julien Green gave us this snatch of dialogue in one of his journals. It requires a lot of honesty to be grateful for the insight behind his barbed words because they expose the dubious nature of so many of our efforts to get rid of our faults. Behind the facade of moral earnestness, the powers that be in the soul are dreaming of a state in which we could at last dissociate ourselves from the common herd who sin. Oh to be so free of faults that we would never need to ask others' forgiveness! Oh to be invulnerable!

As long as pride wants to separate us from others, the Spirit of God has to sabotage our attempts to get rid of sin from our lives. If we continue to fall again and again, at least there is a chance of our breaking through in the end into a humble sense of solidarity with others in their weakness and enter the way of compassion.

Pride (clothed in religious fervor) can attempt to over-power the repeat offenders within the society of our selves and banish the bad habits, embarrassing slips, and persist-ent nasty traits that spoil self-esteem. Or it can try to deny and cover them over through the technique of projection. Then we divert onto others the disapproval and contempt we feel for these "bad elements" within ourselves. We per-mit ourselves to vent our scorn and disappointment in our-selves by condemning others who manifest similar faults. Jesus confronted those of us trapped in this cycle of projec-tion with words of cutting irony: "You hypocrite, first take the log out of your own eye, and then you will see clearly to take the speck out of your brother's eye" (Matthew 7:5).

Nothing helps unless we are prepared to meet the repeat offenders within ourselves and let the Spirit intro-duce us to these elements who again and again ruin our record. Just to know them, and to know ourselves as pow-erless to reform them through our own strength, is to make a great stride through the narrow gate that leads to life. The classic spiritual guides try to impress on us the power of this recognition, this breakthrough to humility.

"He who sees himself as he is, and has seen his sin, is greater than the one who raises the dead," St. Isaac the Syrian taught. When we are prepared to face our besetting faults, then the opportunity comes for the Spirit to change our practice of scorning, punishing, and loathing weak-ness. "Purity of heart," St. Isaac goes on, "is love for those who fall. If you see your brother in the act of sinning throw about his shoulders the mantle of your love."[5] Love for those who fall can only be learned by loving those who fall within our own inner community of selves. But how on earth can we show love for ourselves in our falling without condoning and inflaming those faults that pain God and injure our neighbor? What is this loving that heals rather than worsens our recidivism?

The saints teach a practice of loving our selves in our failing, an actual art we can all learn with patience. It is so simple that their recommendation offends those who believe that complicated wrestling and psychological probing of our failings must necessarily be involved in our conversion. Like Naaman the Syrian, who was disgusted by the straightforwardness of Elisha's prescription for his leprosy, they need persuasion actually to embark on the practice the saints recommend. It consists in ministering the forgiveness of God to our faults instantly and repeatedly without fretting:

> Every time you fall into some pardonable transgression, even if it happens a thousand times a day, as soon as you notice it, do not torture yourself and so waste your time without profit, but at once humble yourself and, conscious of your weakness, turn to God with hope and call to Him from the depths of your heart: "O Lord, my God! I have done this because I am what I am and so nothing can be expected of me but such transgressions or even worse, if Thy grace does not help me and I am left to myself alone. I grieve over what I have done, especially because my life has no righteousness responding to Thy care of me, but I continue to fall and to fall. Forgive me and give me the strength not to offend Thee again and in no way to digress from Thy will. For I zealously wish to work for Thee, to please Thee and be obedient to Thee in all things." When you have done this, do not torment yourself with thoughts as to whether God has forgiven you. The Lord is near and listens to the sighing of His servants. So calm yourself in this certainty and, having regained your calm, continue your usual occupations as though nothing had happened. You must do this not once but, if necessary, a hundred times and every minute, and the last time with the same perfect trust and daring towards God as the first. In doing this you will tender due honor to the

infinite goodness of God, Whom you must always see as full of infinite loving-kindness towards us.[6]

The obstinate repeat offenders in our inner society, in the meantime before grace accomplishes their rehabilitation, can do us a strange service. If we respond to every fresh offense by a renewed act of daring trust in the infinite loving-kindness of God, then we shall grow in faith. We shall also find ourselves doing the same for the repeat offenders among our neighbors as we are learning to do for ourselves. When our exasperating, recalcitrant sisters and brothers fall and fall again, it will occur to us more and more to throw about their shoulders the mantle of our love. We will be a little closer to grasping the hospitality of God.

Counselor, Spirit of truth, teach me how to forgive my brother and sister not "seven times, but seventy times seven." I itch to correct and control their behavior, it maddens me that their faults are so ingrained. I long to punish or mock them. My inmost feelings spell out curses on them. Nothing will change as long as I either curse or cover over my own habitual slips. The habit of turning after every fall instantly to the Lord asking for forgiveness, the resilience to do this time and time again, is not going to be easy to acquire. I need the special impulse of your grace to start now and to keep doing it.

MEDITATION

Then Peter came and said to him, "Lord, if another member of the church sins against me, how often should I forgive? As many as seven times?" Jesus said to him, "Not seven times, but, I tell you, seventy times seven."

Matthew 18:21–22

Saturday

THOSE OTHER
CHRISTIANS

What would it mean for me to become myself a sign of the oneness of God's church? Of course I join in the usual laments over the separation of the churches but complaints are cheap. My sentiments of ecumenical good-will camouflage my hidden satisfaction that "our sad divisions" allow me to keep my distance from those other Christians with whom I would rather not keep company. There are other Christians whose style, traditions, convictions, and practices repel and upset me. I simply wish they were not there to disturb my sense of the superiority of my own church or circle. The virulence with which Christians hammer away at one another in controversy, or the coolness with which they hold one another at arm's length depresses me, and yet the truth is I am sometimes guilty of both. I am myself a sign of the disunity of God's church.

Nothing will change unless I recognize that my aversions to so many other Christians may be revealing ways in which I am afraid of embracing the fullness of Christian faith. My sin is to confuse the part with the whole. I have embraced certain elements of Christianity and these I claim to be the whole picture. But those other Christians for whom I have contempt or whom I regard as alien may represent authentic dimensions of the whole gospel and the full faith that I am afraid to embrace. I make enemies of them in my heart in order to repudiate, instead of inte-grating into my own life the truths and gifts they represent.

The true change of heart that the Spirit seeks to bring about in this season goes much deeper than cheap resolu-tions to be more charitable about Christians whose ways are different from our own. Tolerance is merely a way of preserving the status quo. The Spirit comes to us in the very persons of those other Christians, asking us to face the challenge of what they represent and stretch the capacity of our minds and hearts in order to make room for it in our own lives of faith.

What is the Spirit trying to show you now about your aversions to other Christians? Today all over the world, wherever believers are letting down their defenses in prayer, the Spirit is expanding their grasp of the fullness of the gospel. People who were nervous about "bringing reli-gion into politics," and prejudiced against liberation the-ologians and radicals, are recognizing that for God's will to be done on earth as in heaven, ordinary Christians have to practice persistent, concrete struggles against the prin-cipalities and powers that operate behind the benign facades of governments, corporations, and newspaper offices. Pragmatic types for whom social action in the name of Christ was the only thing that mattered, who regarded spirituality with suspicion, are beginning to hear the call to holiness and intimacy with God. Those who would have dismissed Eastern Orthodox Christianity as archaic and merely exotic are discovering the depths of wisdom and knowledge of God found in its traditions. Christians who used to laugh at those caught up in the charismatic movement are acknowledging their own poverty of fervor, and opening themselves to a new aware-ness of the power of the indwelling Spirit.

Roman Catholics are falling in love with the scriptures. Evangelicals are discovering the converting power and centrality of the Holy Eucharist. Fundamentalists who used to condemn theologians for undermining the faith are relaxing their fears and exploring the world opened up by biblical criticism. Those under the banner of "the faith once delivered to the saints" who feared the inroads of liberal thinkers are taking courage in the Spirit to reckon with the challenges of new knowledge in a changing world. Traditionalists who were scandalized by the very notion of feminism are finding scales failing from their eyes. Protestants are discovering the Virgin Mary, liberals are experiencing the healing ministry. . . . Where could we end?

Thomas Merton was deeply impressed by a profound and simple statement of an Orthodox bishop, Metropolitan Eulogius: "People like St. Seraphim, St. Francis, and many others have accomplished the unity of the churches in their own lives." He took this as a clue to his own vocation as a monk:

> If I can unite *in myself* the thought and devotion of Eastern and Western Christendom, the Greek and the Latin Fathers, the Russian with the Spanish mystics, I can prepare in myself the reunion of divided Christians. From that secret and unspoken unity in myself can eventually come a visible and Manifest unity of all Christians. . . . We must contain all divided worlds in ourselves and transcend them in Christ.[7]

Of course I will always be a Christian in a particular tradition, with the gifts and the weaknesses that mark it. But I belong to the one, holy, catholic, and apostolic church. I must delight in calling myself a catholic Christian. The title "catholic" is not the possession of a denomination or a party but a name that expresses the all-embracing and universal character of the church. If the church is catholic, and not another of humankind's splinter groups, then I am catholic for "each of the faithful is a little church." I am called to be a sign of the unity in diversity that the Spirit is striving to build and restore.

Today the Spirit is asking me to make more room in myself for the fullness of the gospel by taking to heart the witness of other Christians whom I have been content to regard as foreign. Who are they? What are they showing me? What would I have to do to incorporate that into my own life?

Spirit of God, give me the courage to take stock of the prejudices, indifference, and hostility that cause me to keep at arm's length or belittle those other Christians whose ways and convictions alarm or baffle me. If I weighed these prayerfully I would probably find that I am afraid of incorporating into my life the strengths and truths you have given to these brothers and sisters of mine. I cling onto my partial vision and limited response instead of exploring the catholicity of Christian experience. How will you help me overcome my fears of what these other Christians represent?

MEDITATION
John 17   Ephesians 2:11–22

For he is our peace; in his flesh he has made both groups into one and has broken down the dividing wall, that is, the hostility between us. He has abolished the law with its commandments and ordinances, that he might create in himself one new humanity in place of the two, thus making peace, and might reconcile both groups to God in one body through the cross, thus putting to death that hostility through it.

Ephesians 2:14–16

The Fourth
Week of Lent

Monday

DOMINEERING VIRTUES

*"Truly I tell you, the tax collectors and the prostitutes
are going into the kingdom of God ahead of you."
(Matthew 21:31)*

These words of Jesus to the devout Jewish authorities stick to us like burrs. These men were disciplined and learned. We do not like the suggestion that unruly and "unhealthy" elements might be more responsive to God's good news than the virtuous and strong. The implication that established virtues, rather than sins, might hold us back from entering the new community of God makes us uncomfortable. The Counselor, intent on teaching us all things, insists on bringing to our remembrance all that Christ has said to us, especially these kinds of subversive words that call into question the spiritual status quo in the community of selves.

We all have strengths and virtues. And these strengths and virtues can come to commandeer the positions of power in our lives and deny the rights of other elements within our make-up. For example, some good and gifted people tend to be manipulative and domineering. They keep their virtues going at the high price of putting down other sides of themselves, and they reproduce this in their relationships with other people. They seem integrated enough, but the integration is simulated because they have merely retreated into their strengths. The aspects of themselves they repudiate are not necessarily difficult or sinister, either; virtues can oppress aspects of ourselves that are vital constituents of our real goodness.

Meditating upon the story of Martha and Mary recorded in the tenth chapter of St. Luke's gospel can help us identify these workings of the politics of the heart. Nowhere in the gospels is it suggested that Martha is other than a truly good woman. "Jesus loved Martha...," John writes in his gospel. She makes herself busy serving. She is used to going all out to please others, and there is no one she is more anxious to please than her friend the prophet. But her busyness is not peaceful and resentment boils over. "Lord, do you not care that my sister has left me to do all the work by myself?"

Martha has identified herself completely with her talents for serving. On this occasion she takes for granted that the "only way to be" with Jesus is to serve him an elaborate meal. But this is not true. Of course there are other ways, such as simply sitting and relishing his company and using this golden opportunity to learn more from him. Mary's choice of this way upsets Martha because it gives the lie to the decree of her dictatorial virtue that "you can't go wrong if you are serving others." Martha tries to make Jesus feel guilty and send Mary to help her. Then her virtue will feel secure again in its monopoly of approval. Jesus refuses to play her game and contradicts the monopolizing claims of Martha's virtue. In this case it has led her astray. Jesus is taking the radical step of training women—women!—to be his disciples and assistants. Mary has chosen to sit at the master's feet as an apprentice and deepen her knowledge of the kingdom in his company. No one has the right to interfere with her vocation.

The story resonates with many people because Martha's distraction with much serving suggests one of the most common compulsions of modern life. Addiction would not be too strong a word to describe the need of many of us to be constantly productive and active. We have been brought up to assume that busying ourselves incessantly in fulfilling people's wants and needs will guarantee their approval. We have certainly discovered that stopping sets off shrill voices of disapproval inside us that will not desist until we start working again. The church is rife with addicts to "much serving." It is a place where tyrannical virtues can get away with murder, or if not with murder, can get away with repression of the contemplative. There are not many churches where "the good portion" is defended and encouraged, where people are trained in ways of developing their own intimacy with Christ and knowledge of God so that they can bring others to share what they have experienced.

The story ends abruptly with Jesus' words of challenge to Martha. I wonder what happens next. In my imagination I feel Martha's cheeks burning and sense her confusion as she responds to Jesus' gesture inviting her to sit with Mary. She listens as Jesus picks up the thread of his teaching and her heart slows down. She has to struggle to shake off anxiety about certain of her dishes that must surely be burning or going to waste by now. But simply by sitting she finds herself intrigued by Jesus' message again and, almost in spite of herself, starts to memorize the most pithy of his sayings. Later on, as the three of them discuss a new parable over the one course Jesus asked for, she realizes she too can be a student and confidante of Jesus, not only the perfect hostess.

Spirit of truth, I tend to assume that self-examination is exclusively a matter of detecting my failings so I can confess them to God. This is all very well, and you inspire me to do it. In fact I should do it more thoroughly and more often. But I wonder whether I am sometimes behaving like those mother birds who, when hunters approach their nest, pretend to be wounded by dragging a wing in order to lure them away from their chicks. I play the penitent in order to distract attention from what I do not want disturbed, namely my virtues and strengths. If I let you hold these up to the light perhaps I would see how I invest so much in them that I sacrifice all sorts of other important potentialities to their demands. I would have to admit that my virtues can bully other aspects of my true self. How often I see intellectual people stifling their feelings and being contemptuous when others display emotions. How common it is for pragmatic people to avoid deep thought and show impatience with those who want to explore the meaning of actions. If I look within myself, with your gentle light, I am certain to find evidence of similar intolerance of others who represent undeveloped aspects of my own self.

MEDITATION
Luke 10:38–42

You may feel drawn to enter the story of Martha and Mary using your imagination to experience it through the eyes of Mary. See whether you can share her feelings of being supported and encouraged by Jesus after being told she had no right to be doing what she is doing.

You could then ask whether there is some aspect of your own self that is often bullied by your stronger selves, some part that Jesus wants to support and vindicate. For example, do you hear voices within you asserting that life is just too busy to give time for reading, for prayer, for retreat . . . ? What is going on?

Tuesday

I CAN LIVE WITH MYSTERY AND THE UNKNOWN

F ear of the unknown" is a common expression in which wisdom is dressed in her everyday clothes. Our almost instinctive response to the unknown is fear rather than trust. We do not feel safe until we know what we are encountering. But human beings are so varied in race, language, culture, and religion, and differences in gender and personal experience are so significant that we are to a vast extent strangers to one another. Fear of what we do not understand in others prevents us from being in community with them. We have a need to exclude them from community, which we assume has to consist of the more or less like-minded. Yet it is rare for us to have the honesty to admit that the reason we reject relationship with those different from ourselves is that we fear the unknown in them. Instead we find reasons for rejecting them. We project onto the blankness of the unknown in them a pseudo-understanding of our own. We think we know what makes them tick, and that usually justifies our staying out of relationship with them. More often than not the imaginary knowledge of the stranger we use as a pretext for rejection is not an invention of our own. Society has a vast stock-in-trade of folklore, prejudices, and pseudo-science on which we draw automatically in categorizing others to negate their strangeness.

In the face of our deep-rooted bias against the unknown, God must be mad to try and create a universal community, a catholic church. It was mad to try to turn human beings round from this fear of the unknown in each other. But that is the message of the cross—the "foolishness of God." God was mad enough to release into our world a perfect love that casts out fear and goes on preventing us from settling for our denominations, cliques, sects, and cultural enclaves. In the kingdom the Spirit grapples with our fear of the unknown in one another until strangers can let go and enter into relationship with one another in reciprocal respect for the mystery of each other.

People think that the Spirit, in leading us into all truth, is going to fill our heads with all sorts of knowledge. Nothing could be further from the truth. Our heads are already full of what we think is knowledge of others but is largely groundless and false. Being "in the truth" depends on our readiness not only to unlearn bit by bit the prejudices we have against one another, but also to surrender the very tendency itself of pretending to know about others what we do not know. The truth into which the Spirit is striving to lead us is a much barer, simpler place, a place of greater unknowing, than we imagine. In that place we learn to love what we do not yet know.

Those of us who are called by God to the ministry of spiritual direction and counseling spend long hours "listening others into speech," trying to create a climate of hospitality for their unique and often secret patterns of experience in order to help them recognize how God is keeping company with them. As others risk the sharing of hidden feelings and memories, we are repeatedly struck by the injustice of our superficial judgments of others. Hearing the first sacramental confession of a woman whom I know to be dismissed by most as a neurotic, for example, I learn a history of suffering and struggle completely unsuspected by those who think their snap judgments justify their scorn of her. "If only people knew..." I murmur to myself as men and women take me round to the back of their lives. It is a humbling work in which every effort to understand others for the sake of helping them know themselves and God must be cleansed of pride and force. In the words of Carl Jung:

> Understanding is a fearful binding power, at times a veritable murder of the soul as soon as it flattens out vitally important differences. The core of the individual is a mystery of life which is snuffed out when it is "grasped."... True understanding seems to me to be one which does not understand, yet lives and works.[1]

Of course there is no possibility of respecting the mystery of others if we have not learned to respect our own. Assuming what we know of ourselves to be the whole truth, we turn with equal confidence to our labeling of others. But within the society of selves there are the unknown ones. The truth is that our assessment of our own characters, our knowledge about why we act and feel as we do, is partial and fragmentary. The most searching psychoanalysis, the most assiduous self-examination can only yield so much and beyond that lies the "yet unknown" of the soul. Truth is what God knows, and we do not yet know what God knows about us and our place in the whole web of life. Everything less than what God knows is not the whole truth.

The mystery of ourselves is the history of God with us. God is in everything in me and everything I do as partner, victim, sovereign, fellow-sufferer, source of life . . . but how little I know of that yet! Judgment will be the revelation of how the Trinity has been with me at the meeting-place of all my relationships. In the judgment I will have to surrender every one of the illusions I have spun around me, and open every dark place in me to the light. judgment will be the disclosure of how God has been with everyone else: the mind reels at the prospect of having to compare what we thought we knew of others and what God knew. Only then will the communion of saints finally come.

Holy Spirit, the more I contemplate your life in my heart, and Christ whom you make present within me, the more presumptuous my so-called self-knowledge seems. I am as much a mystery as you are! "The wind blows where it chooses, and you hear the sound of it, but you do not know where it comes from or where it goes. So it is with everyone who is born of the Spirit" (John 3:8). As I seek to understand myself let me leave room for the hidden selves whom you alone know. The more I acknowledge the unknown in myself the less fear I will have of the unknown in my neighbors. The more I revere the mystery of your life in me, the more prepared I will be to treat others, too, as bearers of mystery, and be in communion with them. I cannot love my neighbor unless I get used to letting love go where knowledge cannot penetrate. Prayer is the place where I can practice loving without knowing. For Christ is known and yet unknown to me and I love him. Help me love without restraint him whom my understanding cannot grasp.

MEDITATION

Think of someone you look down on. Pray to Christ living in his or her heart. Consider all that you do not know
about that person, the family history, the secret struggles,
the hidden graces, the concealed achievements. Ask
Christ to admit you into his love and hope for her or him.
Confess and hand over your prejudices.

Wednesday

ALL THE SICK

*Jesus went throughout Galilee, teaching in their syna-
gogues and proclaiming the good news of the kingdom
and curing every disease and every sickness among the
people. So his fame spread through out all Syria, and
they brought him all the sick, those who were afflicted
with various diseases and pains, demoniacs, epileptics,
and paralytics, and he cured them. (Matthew 4:23–24)*

If I were to tear out of the gospels the pages in which
Jesus is dealing with the sick and possessed there would
only be a few leaves left; otherwise I might be tempted to
try. Praying the gospels involves keeping a lot of company
with the diseased and mad, which is why so many
Christians find reasons for not doing it. They need to cling
onto their sense of health and sanity, and they have to pay
the price of keeping their distance from Jesus whom the

gospels portray so constantly surrounded by the sick. To experience his nearness means that we must find ourselves among the sick in need of the physician. If the Healer dwells in the heart we need to bring to him all the sick among the many selves of the self.

Can I find within myself a demoniac? Well, I know that I am not "possessed by the devil" in the strict sense. But I have to recognize pockets of craziness in my make-up and my nightmares compel me to recognize that I harbor strange savages and victims within. It is good to bring to Christ in prayer each experience of these terrors of the night. It is right to lessen the distance I put between myself and those who have lost their sanity.

But the image of the demoniac may give me access to other parts of myself that I would not normally consider as diseased. The demoniacs in the scriptures represent the way the human heart can be penetrated by what is alien and inhuman. We are vulnerable to being invaded and manipulated by irrational forces that seek to tear community apart and force people into isolation and competition. The Greek word for "devil" derives from a root meaning "to divide." The demonic is what seeks to tear the thousand threads that link us in God to one another, forcing people into isolation and competition, confining them to what is illusory and lifeless.

What would be mad is for me to pretend that I am immune to this penetration by the inhuman forces of separation, that not one part of me has been recruited by the "liar and father of lies." No sheltered life can shut out the insidious influence of the lies that infest human societies, and the laboratory conditions of the hermit life prove that even solitude is no escape from them.

The Christ who dwells in you is the man who had an agonizing struggle in the wilderness to resist being penetrated by the demonic forces of untruth. In the power of the Holy Spirit he liberated thousands of people who had been disconnected from their health and relationships by these forces. In the power of the same Spirit he seeks to liberate those parts of yourself that have been penetrated by falsehood and recruited for the campaign against the new community of the kingdom. Exorcism is for most modern people a baffling relic from a superstitious past, and it is almost impossible for them to understand what was going on in the ministry of Jesus. But all of us can take the gospel exorcisms at the very least as dramatic symbols for Christ's power to emancipate human lives from the grip of what is foreign to, and destructive of, our health, freedom, and solidarity. Face Christ in your own heart and consent to his ministry of exorcism now. There are in you pockets of resistance to the kingdom and the Spirit, places where falsehood has dug in. Warped convictions and diseased attitudes are very tenacious. They will not surrender easily.

> What have you to do with us, Jesus of Nazareth?
> Have you come to destroy us? I know who you are,
> the Holy One of God. (Mark 1:24)

The difficulty is that the most profoundly diseased and demonic notions and attitudes that pervade the world and infest our hearts are so common and deep-seated that they appear normal. They seem natural, though they are in violent contradiction with the created nature God endowed us with; they have become, as we say, "second nature." Those things which Christ yearns to eliminate from us with a new "Be silent, and come out of him!" are the attitudes that most people take for granted as normal.

The demoniacs within us are not raving lunatics, but those persons in our inner community who are racist, who behind a polite mask nurse condescension and contempt towards those of other cultures, races, and color. They are the selves who maintain in the heart hostile stereotypes, for example, of Jews as despicable and homosexuals as contemptible and dangerous, so that as Christians we perpetuate, instead of resist, vile ancient prejudices. They are the selves who cling to the ancient glamorization of war, and accept without a murmur the preparations for nuclear warfare that can destroy the earth. They are the inner persons who are the collaborators with the forces of consumerism and waste. The demoniacs within may be the most conservative parts of ourselves that are scared of any change in the balance of power, that flare up, sickened and panicky, as, for example, women the world over collectively question the subordinate roles they have been assigned in church and society for generations and begin to choose together to change them. Christ means to meet and confront all these perverted parts of ourselves and liberate them through the touch of the Spirit from their captivity to the "world-rulers of this darkness." If we refuse to bring them to him we may find ourselves identified with the Pharisees in John's story of the healing of the man born blind.

"Surely we are not blind, are we?" Jesus said to them, "If you were blind, you would not have sin. But now that you say, 'We see,' your sin remains." (John 9:40–41)

Spirit of freedom, jolt me out of complacency. Some of my prejudices and convictions are utterly incompatible with the vulnerable, suffering, but victorious love of God revealed in the cross of Jesus. They are alien and false but because they are so taken for granted in the world I excuse them in myself. Help me bring those diseased parts of me that are occupied by lies one by one to Christ so that he can liberate them through your life-giving touch.

MEDITATION

> But if it is by the spirit of God that I cast out
> demons, then the kingdom of God has come to you.
>
> *Matthew 12:28*

They went to Capernaum; and when the sabbath came, he entered the synagogue and taught. They were astounded at his teaching, for he taught them as one having authority, and not as the scribes. Just then there was in their synagogue a man with an unclean spirit, and he cried out, "What have you to do with us, Jesus of Nazareth? Have you come to destroy us? I know who you are, the Holy One of God." But Jesus rebuked him, saying, "Be silent, and come out of him!" And the unclean spirit, convulsing him and crying with a loud voice, came out of him. They were all amazed, and they kept on asking one another, "What is this? A new teaching—with authority! He commands even the unclean spirits, and they obey him."

Mark 1:21–28

Thursday

REJOICE WITH THOSE WHO REJOICE

Paul uses a simple metaphor for the gift of the Spirit, taken from everyday commercial practice. "He who has prepared us for this very thing is God, who has given us the Spirit as a guarantee" (2 Corinthians 5:5). The word translated "guarantee" was used by merchants to describe a free sample sent in advance of the main delivery to assure the buyer of the quality of the merchandise. It was also the word for a down-payment. Paul must have used it many times in writing out invoices for his business.

Our experience of the Spirit is just a beginning. As our hearts expand and become more hospitable and compassionate the Spirit will fill us more. But it is only on the other side of death that we can experience the ultimate rending and remaking, the stretching and opening that will allow us to receive the Spirit in all its fullness. Only through that expansion and flowering will we be able to participate in the communion of saints in which everything that belongs to each will belong to all. We cannot pretend to imagine what unrestricted sharing of life with one another will be like. The mystics tell of experiences in prayer in which in being united with God they feel united with all living brings. These seem to be foretastes of this ultimate community of life, and their words, paradoxical and halting as they are, resonate so deeply within some of us that we answer quietly: "Yes, this is what we are made for, this is where we are heading."

Paul's image of the Spirit in the heart as a free sample or down-payment is remarkably unmystical and unromantic. It helps me realize that it is not in otherworldly intimations that I will be given a foretaste of the communion of saints that is our destiny and fulfillment, but rather in down-to-earth experiences in daily life. Paul tells us simply: "Rejoice with those who rejoice, weep with those who weep" (Romans 12:15). It is by practicing empathy with our neighbors, allowing our hearts to resonate in tune with their experience, letting their lives flow into ours, and ours into theirs. It is by practicing the everyday arts of the common life that we prepare for what is to come.

What happens when we try to put this invitation into practice? The strange thing is that we experience the cross even in trying to rejoice with those who rejoice. We begin to realize that to rejoice with people other than personal friends and relatives goes against the grain of the times. Modern western culture exalts private life and encourages people to pursue their own goals and satisfactions on their own, or within the confines of the family. The joys and sorrows of others are their affair; what has the joy of strangers to do with me? Community has crumbled away. The shared life, which is God's design for us, has become for millions simply a weird and unreal idea. Even within churches openness to the joy of others is not cultivated everywhere. Many Christians regard the church merely as a venerable agency for providing services of worship, certain pastoral facilities, and good works. It would never occur to them that the common life Paul spoke of—"if one member suffers, all suffer together with it; if one member is honored, all rejoice together with it" (1 Corinthians 12:26)—is meant to be realized in actuality in the church.

As I try to rejoice with those who rejoice I realize I cannot do so unless I crucify within myself attitudes of separation from and indifference to others that the world takes for granted as perfectly sound, and that the church absorbs.

Then I discover that the attempt to rejoice with those who rejoice exposes my envy and jealousy. To rejoice simply because another has succeeded, or has been rewarded, or has been blessed with good fortune, even when one's own life is not affected in the least, is to break free of self-centeredness. But I have not done that. When others have cause to rejoice I often react with self-pity because my life seems wanting by comparison. Sometimes I resent the fulfillment of others and have to feign congratulation. I think they do not deserve to have occasions for joy. To participate in the joy of others purely for their sake is to crucify envy and the spirit of calculation that is so utterly foreign to God who "is kind to the ungrateful and the wicked" (Luke 6:35).

The fitfulness and shallowness of my attempts to rejoice with those who rejoice reveals the painful truth that I am out of practice in rejoicing over God's gifts in my own life. I cannot rejoice with those who rejoice unless I am adept in recognizing occasions in my daily life for celebration, praise, and thanksgiving. The more grudging, skeptical, and negative I am about my own lot and path, the less will I be able to take part in others' joys. I must learn to rejoice in God's gifts to me. Unless I "practice the scales of rejoicing" over my own life, I will be unable to join the chorus when it comes to the joys of strangers and my neighbors.

The expression "practicing the scales of rejoicing" is a gift of the poet W. H. Auden. It helps me accept that before the art of celebrating the gifts of God becomes second nature to me I need to practice. For now my clumsy attempts must sound to the ears of the angels as awkward and unmusical as the sounds of a beginner's piano practice do to us.

In scripture, joy is constantly associated with the experience of the Holy Spirit. "At that same hour Jesus rejoiced in the Holy Spirit and said, 'I thank you, Father, Lord of heaven and earth'" (Luke 10:21). The Spirit is the joy of the Godhead. The Spirit is the joy of God in a magnificent creation still unfolding. The Spirit is the joy of God in us, male and female in the divine image. The Spirit is the joy in heaven that celebrates the repentance of sinners, every movement of response to the love of God and the gift of life. To rejoice with those who rejoice is to open myself to the currents of divine joy that the Spirit generates in flowing between, through, and among us.

Spirit of joy, the fixed smile of the perpetually cheerful Christian, maintained at the expense of so much denial and so much secret fatigue, is not what I am seeking from you. I want to live in the truth that I am bound up with everyone and everything in a single bundle of life. I cannot rejoice with every single one who rejoices, because I am limited. What I ask is for you to break down some more of my resistance to sharing the joy of others, to rejoicing in you with them. What I need is to learn how to praise and celebrate your gifts. I feel incapable, without your special grace, of removing the insulation that prevents my heart from thrilling to all that is good, all that is gift.

MEDITATION

Rejoice in the Lord always; again I will say, Rejoice. Let your gentleness be known to everyone. The Lord is near. Do not worry about anything, but in everything by prayer and supplication with thanksgiving let your requests be made known to God. And the peace of God, which surpasses all understanding, will guard your hearts and your minds in Christ Jesus.

Finally, beloved, whatever is true, whatever is honorable, whatever is just, whatever is pure, whatever is pleasing, whatever is commendable, if there is any excellence and if there is anything worthy of praise, think about these things. Keep on doing the things that you have learned and received and heard and seen in me, and the God of peace will be with you.

Philippians 4:4–9

Friday

WEEP WITH THOSE WHO WEEP

Our reluctance to weep with those who weep has many causes. Sometimes we refuse to get involved with those who grieve because we could do something to alleviate the anguish, but we are not prepared to pay the cost. We pass by on the other side. Yet, oddly, we are just as likely to shun those in grief for the opposite reason, that there is absolutely nothing we can do that can be of any practical help. If I see myself as a helper *par excellence* and depend on doing others good for my own sense of self-esteem, I am likely to keep my distance from those whom I cannot help. Their grief threatens to make me feel powerless.

Tears can unnerve and annoy us. Our impulse is to urge the weepers to stop crying. We ply them with soothing assurances, however groundless, that might stem the flow. "Everything is going to be all right." We find that our tolerance for grieving is limited. A certain point is reached after which we assert that "enough is enough" and start insisting that they "pull themselves together."

Our intolerance is often due to our refusal to face grief in our own hearts. The grief of others threatens to penetrate our defenses and stir up our own neglected and denied sadness. Among the selves of the self there are mourners who grieve over the losses we have sustained. Many of us have been taught to despise these bearers of grief who continue to mourn the loss of loved ones, failures and unrealized dreams, rejections and disappointments. We rail at them as agents of self-pity. We scorn them as useless, scolding them for pointless raking up of the past if they escape from the basement of the heart and display to our dominant selves wounds and memories of sadness and loss. We are embarrassed by their persistence. We had hoped they would fade away as we grew older. We know that Jesus in the Beatitudes congratulated those who mourn, and promised that they would be comforted. But we insist that this particular Beatitude has no application to us. We need to maintain that we have nothing to grieve about.

Before we can weep with those who weep we need to do two things. First we need to see whether we have allowed ourselves to weep for ourselves. There comes a point in the lives of countless adults when their relationship with God and their growth in freedom and compassion depends on allowing themselves to mourn their own losses and allowing God to touch them in grief. I have found again and again that repentance involves not so much turning from sins as letting go of the deep-seated habit of stoicism, the relentless forced march of putting one's best foot forward. The tears that pour from people making their first sacramental confession are seldom tears of shame. They are usually tears of lament, mourning over hurt, their own hurt and the hurting they did out of their hurt. Sometimes the tears have had to wait twenty-five years to be cried.

We need to come to the truth about tears themselves. Tears are difficult to understand if we probe them with masculine logic and insist on knowing what they mean and what good they are. The scientists have not been able to fathom the purpose of tears, though a little evidence has come to light recently that they actually flush certain chemicals out from the system, affording relief. Tears are a mystery, and to trust them involves a measure of surrender, especially for men. Tears are tears. The great tradition of spirituality speaks of a gift of tears that comes from God, a manifestation of the grief that makes for joy—about which we thought some weeks ago. If we adamantly refuse to weep we are fighting our humanity; we are certainly grieving the Holy Spirit.

"Jesus wept." This is the briefest utterance of scripture about the Lord, and one of the most forgotten and neg-lected. We need to meditate on the grieving of Jesus, look-ing into a face streaming with tears. If we look away from this face, we are turning away from him as he is. We are refusing the truth of his humanity and ours.

Accepting Christ grieving with us in our grief. Accepting Christ grieving with the world in which he now lives and moves in his secret risen presence. Accepting Christ grieving with those who weep now, and weeping with them with him. Most of us have hardly begun to accept him in tears.

"Weep with those who weep." If we do we shall learn that tears are a sign of our deep unity in God. We shall discover that tears are signs of sacrifice and sharing through which love lifts suffering by distributing it to others who are ready for it.

God forbid we should imagine that it is only the saints, or only Christians who know this. Robert Kegan, a noted authority in the psychology of human development, recalls in his book *The Evolving Self* an evening spent with Rifka, a Jewish mother in the Hasidic community. Rifka is explaining that she is not a strict Hasid since she is prepared at a pinch to shop at the local supermarket, which is not kosher. She tells in her rich Yiddish accent how she had rushed there recently to get some butter when her son Louis had turned up unexpectedly with his girlfriend. That night she had not been able to sleep. It was because she had seen a woman with a retarded child in the supermarket.

> "And then witout—I mean I din't do it myself, I started to cry. And I cried. I cried for that mother vhat had an idiot vhat kept on living. I cried for that mother vhat had an idiot and vhass pricing the mustard. And I cried for the idiot what whass life. He vhass life."
>
> "It's terrible," I mumbled, not knowing what to say.
>
> "Don't say this. Vhat is terrible?" she said, "I'm telling you should know. I'm talking to you. That woman, that mother, ve did not say a word to each other, but ve talked. Not till I came home vhass many hours later did I know ve talked. But ve talked, What is terrible? You live, ve talked. And you know what I thought when I vhass crying? I thought: 'I cry tonight now this mother vit her idiot what is so beautiful, vhat is life, tomorrow she vill cry less.'"[2]

Spirit of God, water of life, you are the tears of God. Help me weep with those who weep, as well as rejoice with those who rejoice. Help me be less afraid to mourn what I have lost in my own life so that I can keep others company in theirs. In keeping company with them I will be with Christ. From him will come the comfort he has promised when the time comes.

MEDITATION
John 11:1–44
Let Christ in grief come alive for you in prayer by meditating on the story of the raising of Lazarus.

> When Jesus saw her weeping, and the Jews who came with her also weeping, he was deeply moved in spirit and troubled.... Jesus wept.
>
> *John 11:33–35, RSV*

Saturday

THE BURDEN-
BEARER

It was pouring with rain as the bus pulled up in Nazareth and I was happy. Lancashire folk are used to rain and it made me feel at home. The bus set me down outside an open shopfront and the first person I saw was...a young bearded carpenter in his late twenties carrying a large plank over his shoulder! It was another of those coincidences that make me feel that God sometimes wants to be playful, and I shook my finger at God, saying: "No tricks, please, no more special effects!"

The need to shelter from the rain that day gave me ample time for meditation and the image of the burden-bearer returned to me again and again. Sipping Turkish coffee in a café I thought of Christ and the paradox of his summoning us to take up the cross and follow him, while claiming that his yoke is easy and his burden light. In the marketplace I met one of the Little Sisters of Jesus, who share the lives of the poorest of the poor. I asked her permission to spend some time in the chapel where Charles de Foucault, who inspired their way of life, prayed during his hidden years as a menial in the service of the Poor

Clares. I was grateful that she overcame her initial reluctance and took me there.

It was one of the most powerful places of prayer I have been in. Kneeling on the rush matting, I felt drawn into a vortex of care centered on the altar. Christ seemed to be drawing to himself the sufferings and needs of the world through the sisters kneeling in prayer. "Bear one another's burdens, and in this way you will fulfill the law of Christ" (Galatians 6:2). These women had dedicated their lives to sharing the burdens of the destitute in slums, deserts, and backwaters all over the world. Here in the chapel through intercession they continued without drama and without romance to take onto themselves in Christ a share of the sins, confusions, and sufferings of the world. I often return in spirit to that chapel when I wonder what the secret is of being a burden-bearer in Christ for others, and find myself murmuring words from a poem by Charles Péguy:

> We needs must take our stand at
>   sorrow's very heart.
> And be firmly placed at the axis of distress,
> And by that sacred need to bear a heavier load,
> And to feel more deeply and go the hardest road
> And receive the evil at its greatest stress.[3]

The secret of being a burden-bearer in Christ must lie in the word "exchange." We must bear one another's burdens and we will not be able to do that if we hang on to our own. Those who make their own the cares and sorrows of others must continually hand over their own burdens so that the heart is light enough and has room enough for a share of our neighbors' and the world's load. This is the sharp significance of the words of Christ that have been worn flat for so many by endless repetition in Anglican worship: "Come unto me, all ye that travail and are heavy laden, and I will refresh you." Unless we ourselves hand over to Christ through prayer our own guilt and preoccupations, unless we confide in our sisters and brothers and accept their help as fellow-members of his Body, our hearts will become congested. The sight of others loaded down will cause us to recoil from them. We cannot afford to let them approach in case they might try to hand over some of their burden to us. We will signal to them, often wordlessly, that they had better keep their troubles to themselves. As for the sorrows of the world, we will develop self-protective habits of indifference, and cultivate the conviction that there is nothing we can do about them.

The law of correspondence in the spiritual life tells us that what we recoil from in others reveals what we recoil from within ourselves. If we are afraid of the burdens of others and feel threatened at the prospect of sharing them, we can be certain that we are refusing to face the burden-bearer within ourselves and are not coming to terms with our own travail. Some people simply deny that they have any burden, and with a specious smile maintain that all is well. But their inability to bear the burdens of others betrays the existence in their interior world of a punished inner person loaded with fear, resentment, secrets, and regrets, who is forced into the dark and denied any access to refreshment.

Others adopt a strategy of interior stoicism, deciding to carry their own load with resignation. There is nothing heroic about it, though; it is a form of possessiveness. They know full well that they carry a load within themselves— guilty secrets, family lies, hatreds, dreads, the clutter of a life's confusions—but they hold on to them as dark riches. They have no intention of getting rid of this furniture of the soul, however horribly uncomfortable it is, because they cannot face the prospect of being despoiled and emptied; God knows who or what would move in, if the space were cleared! Or because they are too proud to let others minister to them.

In Lent we consider renunciation, giving up. The tactics whereby we try to palm off on God the renunciation of desserts and treats, when Christ is summoning us to hand over our burdens, would be defiant indeed were they not so pathetic. The words "Come unto me, all ye that travail and are heavy laden, and I will refresh you" are more than an invitation, they are a command. If we do not obey we will not be able to enter into the exchange of burdens within his Body through which he continues to serve the suffering.

Spirit of Christ, how much I depend on you to restore urgency to invitations of his with which I have become bored. "Come unto me, all ye that travail." I bear them so often—and yawn! As if there were something beneath me about this talk of refreshment, as if it referred to others only, neurotics and unfortunates. Holy Spirit, you move as love through every part of me and it is time I allowed you to bring the burden-bearer within me to Christ to be relieved. Unless I do, the energies you want me to use in sharing the burdens of others will be captive to my self-preoccupation.

MEDITATION

> Cast all your anxiety on him, because he cares for you.
>
> 1 Peter 5:7

Are you carrying any loads that others could help you lay down? What anxieties or preoccupations do you not pray about or share with others? What do you hold on to inside? Do you allow Christ to be the burden-bearer for you? How?

The Fifth
Week of Lent

Monday

YOU ALWAYS HAVE THE POOR WITH YOU

Religious experiences come thick and fast in the streets of New York City. I remember having to turn into St. Thomas Fifth Avenue one cold day in Lent to ask myself: "What have I just done?" I had been rushing along close behind a woman in a sable coat. She stepped so deftly over an obstruction on the pavement. Just as deftly, so did I. It was a homeless man, one of tens of thousands, keeping warm over a grating. This is what you do in Manhattan. You learn to step over the poor. I had a religious experience of our irreligion.

The poor are always with us. The question is whether we are with the poor. "Congratulations to you poor!" proclaimed Jesus in what we call the Beatitudes, a pious term which helps us muffle their impact. But Jesus does not congratulate the poor for accepting their lot and dreaming of heaven. The poor he congratulates are like the widow in his parable who would not take no for an answer in her quest for justice. Jesus issues congratulations not for resignation but for hunger and thirst for righteousness, that is,

God's righteousness, his justice that sets wrongs right. The poor are happy who yearn for justice that will restore to them the share of power, work, food, shelter, and culture that has been denied them. They can begin to call themselves happy because their yearning is God's yearning. With and in them God yearns for right to prevail.

It is not possible to be with God unless we are with God with the poor. The equation is strict. Camels cannot get through the eye of a needle. The rich find it almost impossible to enter the realm of God that is spreading through the announcing of good news to the poor. They exclude themselves not because wealth is necessarily corrupting—many rich people are refined and honorable—but because they cannot be with, that is, on the same side as, the poor. The only way they could cross over to the side of the poor where God is would be by accepting that the destitution of the millions is the result of systemic injustice rather than abstract fate or individual fecklessness, and being conscripted in the divine struggle against it.

The maintenance of wealth depends on strong mechanisms of dissociation from the needy, and forceful convictions that their claims are invalid or their aspirations hopeless. It is disturbing to realize that one does not have actually to be rich oneself to use these same mechanisms and harbor these convictions. Few people wear sables, but many follow in their footsteps. Innumerable people who are not well off at all embrace the attitudes that, according to Jesus, damn those who hold them.

We can hardly call Lent a season for the Spirit of truth if we try to defend our attitudes to poverty from the Spirit's probing. How honest can I allow myself to be? Here with the issue of my solidarity with the poor I will probably have to experience the greatest humbling of my complacency.

One by one I have to seize hold of the lies I use to deny the claims of the poor. In public I repudiate the religion of "pie in the sky when you die." Deep within, I console myself with the thought that the millions who know only

grinding toil will be raised into the life of God in heaven.
My wonder at that—and it is true and consoling—slides
into the place where I am looking for an excuse for doing
nothing about poverty. I take refuge in feelings of impotence. The problems are systemic, vast, the changes necessary so revolutionary, the resistances so colossal...while
I analyze and cultivate my pious hopelessness I can keep
my hand over my wallet. Sometimes, though I would not
dare to say it out loud, I reckon that poverty is actually the
human condition and will never change. There are strata
of affluence and I happen to be in one of them. Real culture can only flourish here and the redistribution of
wealth would drain the life-blood from it. Therefore the
claims of the poor must be resisted, though liberal appearances must be maintained and sympathetic noises made
about the scandal of homelessness, world hunger—and, of
course, I "include them in my intercessions." With such
falsehoods I struggle against the Spirit to keep out of solidarity with the poor.

Even if I were to rid myself of these lies, one funda-
mental barrier could still hold me back. True solidarity
with the poor can never happen if I deny the poverty
within myself. I have to hear the Beatitudes spoken to the
poor within me. And the sure sign that the poor within
me are being allowed to speak is if I am praying out of my
need, and voicing my dependence on God. Jesus' teaching
about prayer is disconcertingly focused on asking, seeking,
knocking. His prime concern was that everyone should
find that place within themselves in which they know
their need of daily bread, mercy, protection from trials that
would break them, deliverance from evil, and in and
beyond these things, simply God.

It has now ceased to surprise me how difficult most
people find it to be needy with God. Sometimes men and
women tell me that they rarely pray for themselves and I
think a few of them want me to conclude that they are
advanced in unselfishness. But (usually in men) it is soul-

endangering evasion or (usually in women) diseased self-effacement. It is easier to intercede for others and pray for just causes than it is to be in God's presence a poor man or woman who is going to die, to be honest about what one dreads and needs. When was the last time you took soundings into the places of your own needs, and expressed them to Jesus, and with Jesus to the Father? How can we enter into the experience of the poor if we flatly deny that there are any poor in our hearts? How can we hear the voices of the poor at home and throughout the world, if we condemn the poor selves of the self to silence and vainly try to draw God's attention away from our nakedness with a display of devotion and altruistic intercessions?

Spirit who anointed Jesus to proclaim good news to the poor, let him speak words of welcome to the poor within me, for I am afraid of my own poverty. Unless you draw me to the place of poverty in my heart and help me surrender my mechanisms of denial I will certainly continue to block my ears to the voices of the poor. Let me recognize Christ in the poor, not only the poor "out there" but the poor in here, and do them justice!

MEDITATION
Matthew 25:31–46

> Come, you that are blessed by my Father, inherit the kingdom prepared for you from the foundation of the world; for I was hungry and you gave me food, I was thirsty and you gave me something to drink, I was a stranger and you welcomed me, I was naked and you gave me clothing, I was sick and you took care of me, I was in prison and you visited me.
>
> *Matthew 25:34–36*

Tuesday

GIFTS PROPERLY AFFIRMED

In directing retreats it is my job to suggest experiments in prayer that I think will create an opportunity for retreatants to experience God's love in a fresh way. One experiment, which uses our consecrated power of fantasy, is this:

> Imagine yourself sitting alone on a favorite stretch of seashore. A stranger approaches along the beach. It is the Lord. As he approaches you become aware of an expression on his face that makes clear that his intention is to thank you for all that you do for him. How do you feel? What does Christ say?...

I watch the retreatant's face carefully as I propose this meditation. The responses are usually strong. Some men and women find themselves at once on the verge of tears at the very idea of Christ showing gratitude to them. Others have a baffled look; they heard my words but the notion that Christ may want to thank them is simply unthinkable. Others become pensive, intrigued; they are intuitively aware that the meditation will take them into unexplored territory in their relationship with Christ.

Then they report what happened. Some people cannot go on with the meditation after the initial stage. Christ for them is the master of limitless demands. They are servants only doing their duty. Thanks do not enter in. But others, after their initial resistance, consent to the meditation; they "hear" Christ naming one by one the good things they do for his Body, their neighbors, community, and family. They hear their gifts named and affirmed with love. The intensity with which they feel appreciated in the prayer reveals unerringly the unsuspected existence within their hearts of a great empty space that was waiting to be filled.

I do not usually argue with those who protest that the idea of Christ wanting to express gratitude to us is fantastic and unwarranted. I simply ask them what they think of people who never thank anybody.

The Spirit "allots to each one individually as the Spirit chooses" graces and ministries from the great range of varieties of gifts. How little we know if we fail to realize that this kindling of gifts in us gives joy to the Spirit, that the nurturing of them is bliss to God, and that every single manifestation of them makes the Spirit-filled Christ within us freshly happy!

Suppose then we imagine our gifted selves as members of our inner society. The question arises whether these gifted selves are honored and encouraged or snubbed and denied. We will find that the question is closely linked with some others. How good are we at recognizing and affirming the gifts of others? How emancipated are we from jealousy and envy? How generous are we in giving thanks and praise to others? How sincere is our delight in what they do well? The truth is that we will never be able to affirm in others what we put down in ourselves. Only if we experience Christ's delight in what we do well through grace will we be able to participate with him in delighting in the different gifts of our sisters and brothers.

The most common mechanism for denying our gifts is simply to refuse to name or recognize them. Vast numbers of Christians simply refuse to know what are the gifts that the Spirit within them is struggling to impart to them and develop towards the building up of the Body of Christ. They use the formulaic protests of false modesty to cover their rejection of responsibility as gifted people—"I am just an ordinary churchgoer, you see." Or they adopt a critical stance that minimizes what they do and is quick to detect flaws and worms in the bud. Or they brush off praise and thanks that others offer, canceling their words of appreciation with remarks like: "Oh, it's nothing, really!"

Conventional piety says that most of us are in danger from pride and that we must repeatedly douse our hearts with the cold water of self-depreciation to keep us humble. Most people I meet are in much greater danger from the corrosion of self-doubt. Even those who boast are really compensating for a deep inner lack of belief in their own gifts. These drenchings we administer to ourselves in the supposed interests of humility only worsen the rust and rot. True humility comes from allowing our own gifts to be properly affirmed. It comes from knowing that the gifts we have for the common good are gifts of the Spirit, not mere accidents, and that God delights in our using them and longs for us to hear the divine "Well done, good and faithful servant!" True humility is the sense of our need for each other for completeness, that my gifts supplement yours, and his complements ours, and theirs make up what is wanting in those others. True humility arises from the vision of our interdependence within the web of life.

In homeopathic medicine the cure is effected by administering remedies which, given to a healthy person, would actually stimulate the symptoms of the disease in question. The cure of souls by the Spirit seems to use the same principle. Our symptoms are jealousy and envy and the chronic tendency to devalue the gifts of others and withhold our appreciation. We seem "too full of ourselves." The Spirit's remedy is to pour into our hearts a deeper and richer sense of our own giftedness, since our pride is only a cover for misgivings and self-hatred. It is only when we really accept God's appreciation of us and know ourselves to be gifted through the Spirit that we can communicate to others the same blessing.

Spirit of love, you know all things, and you know how far I am from being the sort of person who recognizes and affirms and encourages the gifts of others. Yet you insist on calling me to represent Christ to others and to welcome them into his Body in which there are varieties of gifts but the same Spirit! How can I overcome my parsimony, envy, and jealousy so that others will experience through me Christ's affirmation of them? Let me be willing to act on the hunch that my withholding of affirmation from others is a symptom of my own deprivation. For how can I give what I do not allow myself to receive? Encourage me to adopt this strange new form of reluctance that allows my gifted selves to be bathed in the radiance of God's appreciation and thanks.

MEDITATION

Why not try for yourself the meditation exercise of letting Christ lovingly thank you for your use of the gifts he has given you?

Wednesday

THE DOUBTERS

Hearing a woman talk about her prayers I once exclaimed: "You are treating God as though he were an elderly clergyman coming for tea! You hide anything you think might embarrass him and you arrange for your outspoken, skeptical teenager to be conveniently out of the house by the time he arrives." We both laughed. She did not have a teenager; that was the name I found for the doubter in her who was always missing when it came time to pray. Outside her prayer-time he would come back, and she spent a lot of time trying to talk down the voice that questioned God's care and kept on undermining her belief in life beyond death.

"The elderly clergyman" is one of the many idols who have to be retired if we are really to pray rather than play a polite game. Again and again we are humiliated on the spiritual journey by discovering that we have treated God as a touchy stranger whom we can keep in the dark about our true feelings and the interior voices that put us to the test. Faith urges us to give our doubts the chance to emerge into the open and give ourselves the chance to see how God meets and answers them. Even if our faith seems particularly full just now, it is important to keep in prac-tice with giving even little doubts a place in our prayer.

Our doubts may not surge into their full force until we meet the suffering that could lie ahead of us, suffering like bereavement and sickness.

With practice we discover that there are a number of doubters within us, and they are different. To our astonishment we realize that some of them are allies and friends on the journey of faith, not blasphemous enemies. Sometimes in the climate of prayer we discover that certain doubts are like angels, agents of the Spirit of truth who is struggling to strip away from us superstitious and immature beliefs. "Doubting the divinity of Christ" for a time may be the only way the Spirit of Christ can get us to start again from scratch and believe in his total humanity. The divine Christ of many people's conventional faith is a fiction, a demigod, not the man who is the Word made flesh. Doubts about doctrines and moral rules may be the only way the Spirit of truth can get us to move from accepting Christianity at secondhand, to appropriating it for ourselves in the light of our own experience and questions. The Spirit can work better with us even if our faith is stripped right down for a time, than if we are cocooned in a complacent religiosity that we are not prepared to have disturbed.

One of our doubters seems more dangerous. His voice speaks not against this belief or that, but simply asks us to admit that the very existence of a loving God is implausible. He points to the Holocaust, the devastation of the exploding AIDS epidemic, the blood-soaked history of the churches, and asks how long we are going to persist in the venerable fiction that God is love. We do our utmost to suppress him and deny that we have heard this voice from within our own hearts. We pretend that it is what *they* say, the atheists. But if we give room even to this doubter in our prayers we might find ourselves led back to the foot of the cross to hear the agonized cry of Jesus: "My God, my God, why have you forsaken me?"

It is not true that there is obviously a God. It is not true that God is obviously loving. It is not obviously true that the execution of a Galilean carpenter turned exorcist and preacher is the axis on which all human destinies turn. The radical doubter may be a kind of very austere prophet within us whom the Spirit of truth uses to make us face the extent of God's own hiddenness and silence. His counterparts in the world are those honest atheists about whom a friend of mine once said: "I am grateful to my atheist friends; they have taught me not to cheat."

Part of the reason for the pathetic inadequacy of much Christian evangelism and apologetics is that we become so naively habituated to Christianity that we are unable to imagine the world and life seen from the standpoint of the unbeliever. So it may be an urgent matter for the Spirit to get us to attend to the doubters within ourselves. That way we might learn to be with unbelievers where they are, and live with the questions to which they do not yet see the answers in what we preach.

There are other doubters in our inner society whom we need to bring to Jesus in prayer so that he can confront them. These are the doubters who mock our hopes, pour cold water on our trust in God, and tell us to stay with what common sense says is safe and sure. These he needs to challenge and disturb: "Is not this the reason you are wrong, that you know neither the scriptures nor the power of God?" (Mark 12:24); "You of little faith, why did you doubt?" (Matthew 14:31). They are the sick and indigent parts of our self, the survivors of past disappointments and abandonments, who draw on the inner fund of hopelessness that is part of fallen human nature. If neglected and brushed aside, they will spread the infection of self-defeat and resignation in the heart. When we hear their complaints and whispers it is urgent that we bring them to Jesus and specifically ask for healing.

God the Counselor, help me to listen to the doubters within me. Because I am not used to expressing doubt in prayer and feel bound to present to God a good appearance of faith, I will need a special gift of courage to pray some of my doubts. Help me to trust that Jesus knows how to handle each of them. Already it is a bit clearer to me that doubt is not in itself wrong. The doubters in me have a vocation to fulfill. If I stop recoiling from them and give them some respect I might find myself becoming more discerning, less liable to take things on authority, less satisfied with what is conventional. Jesus, inspired by you, sounded the depths of human experience, even to the extent of entering the total darkness of dereliction on the cross. If I make room even for my doubts, I would be able to empathize with those who do not yet believe instead of rejecting them as aliens. And if I did that I would be a better witness of the gospel of the cross.

MEDITATION
Psalm 13   John 20:24–31

Thursday

MALE AND FEMALE

Gradually, as we come to love the Spirit of God, we become aware of a growing delight in diversity, and at the same time a growing passion for unity. The Creator Spirit is the source of the infinite variety in creation, and the life that holds everything together in one. In the new creation in Christ that is underway, the Spirit is the source of the varieties of gifts, varieties of service, varieties of working, and the bond that integrates us into one Body. We cannot walk in the Spirit and not glory in the holiness of difference, distinctions, variety, complementarity, uniqueness. We cannot love the Spirit without being gripped by the truth of the unity of all in the Spirit.

This makes life wonderful, but uncomfortable. As we walk in the Spirit we find ourselves angered and saddened more and more by the world's attempt to suppress diversity and impose uniformity. We become horrified at the way hundreds of precious species of creatures are being annihilated because of the lust for profit. We become disgusted by the imperialism of the powerful nations and corporations that care next to nothing for the cultural integrity, the languages and heritage, of little nations and tribes. We are nauseated by the manipulation of the mass media and advertisers that indoctrinate the public into stock responses and tastes. At the same time we lose patience with the prejudices that fuel hatreds and disunity. We are excruciated by jingoism, snobbery, militarism, and all the various forms of domination of one group over another. Our hearts ache for the weaving of human lives into community. The vision of interdependence and reciprocity and the unity of all in God makes us cry out in outrage at the pronouncements of politicians and pundits that are based on the assumption that life is intrinsically competitive, a race to seize what others will take if we do not grab first.

There is one basic polarity in human experience that tests our conversion to the Spirit's way of affirming diversity and nurturing unity. That is the experience of humanity as male and female. The Spirit searches and tests us to know whether we bear good news in our lives about the way women and men complement one another, whether we are ministers of reconciliation in a world in which so many men and women are locked in conflict, mutual ignorance, and frustration.

"There is no longer Jew or Greek, there is no longer slave or free, there is no longer male and female; for all of you are one in Christ Jesus" (Galatians 3:28). This affirmation cannot mean that men and women are neutered on incorporation into Christ. It can only mean that the barriers and antagonisms between them that are a feature of unredeemed life are being overcome in the sphere where God is making a new creation. The community of the Holy Spirit does not flatten out the distinctiveness of being a man or woman. It is a place where full weight is given to and full delight is taken in the gifts, nuances of sensibility, and divinity-inspired specialty of both. In the Spirit, women who have claimed the authority of their experience as women and men who have entered into the fullness of their calling as men see the divine image expressed in the other and in their union.

In the course of its history the church, more often than not, has been incapable of sustaining the radicalism of this equality and complementarity, and has canonized in its life, theology, and spirituality those very barriers that it was called upon to judge and to heal. Now a great shift in consciousness is taking place all over the world that is exposing the extent to which men have systematically relegated women to an inferior status and repressed the authority and wealth of women's experience. The church is being stirred to reappropriate its pristine vision and dismantle the barriers that have restricted the dynamic interplay between the feminine and the masculine within the new life in Christ.

Shall I be a mistrustful foe, a baffled outsider, or a courageous participant in this exploration?

If I want to play my part in the forging of a new spirituality that does equal justice to women's and men's experience of the divine I will have to use once more the basic law of the heart as microcosm of humanity. We can only truly understand, we can only sympathize with what resonates within ourselves. Each human being has both elements of male and female within his or her self. A woman cannot recognize the shape and form or affirm the validity of a man's way of being in the body and in the world unless she is connected with the masculine pole of her own being, and has claimed her own powers of initiative and authority. A man cannot empathize with women and bless their creativity, nurturing powers, and commitment to the webs of relationship unless he fosters within himself his own feminine identity. Alienation from our own souls, where both aspects of humanity reside, reinforces and is in turn reinforced by the war of the sexes in the world.

The alienation of men from women, the alienation of women from men, is one of the greatest triumphs of evil. The heartbreaking deadness or fretful bitterness of countless marriages makes them a modern Gethsemane where Christ is in agony with his sisters and brothers who wear their lives away in uncomprehending strife. Meeting a woman who knows who she is and what she has to give, and loves what manhood is and brings about, is to experience the power of the Spirit. To know men who are initiated into their manhood and love the feminine, is to feel the working of the Spirit. Do people sense that I am one of these and find me a witness to the new life in Christ? I wonder.

Spirit of love, to sense the alienation of men and women in our time is to be drawn into a great world of suffering. Here multitudes groan in the quest for a redemption that the world cannot give.

I have many gifts to ask from you. I ask for the gift of gratitude for my own gender, my own sexuality. Help me praise God for its opportunities, its way of being, the shape and form of my body, the contours of my mind and feelings. I ask for the gift of reverence for the opposite sex. Purge me of prejudice and willful ignorance that blocks my appreciation for "the other." Give me love to be the bond between us and deepen my empathy. Show me how the other sex embodies gifts and values that are latent in my own heart. Help me realize them within myself so that my own humanity can be full, and not mutilated.

MEDITATION

So God created humankind in his image, in the image of God he created them; male and female he created them.

Genesis 1:27

The divine image and likeness is in our being male *and* female. What do women show us of the being and life of God, as distinct from what men reveal?

Friday

OF ONE BLOOD

The final act that brought down on Jesus' head the accumulated rage of the authorities was his disruption of the temple market. The Court of the Gentiles was intended to proclaim that the God of Israel was the God of all humankind. It ought to have been wide open to welcome visitors of every land who were drawn to worship the One God. In fact it had been taken over as the marketplace for the dealers in sacrificial animals and the money-changers. Gentiles could not but draw the conclusion that it was only in obsolete theory that they were welcome in the House of God, not in practice. Jesus burst into the court and began to overturn the tables, chairs, and cages and to halt the fetching and carrying.

> He was teaching and saying, "Is it not written, 'My house shall be called a house of prayer for all the nations'? But you have made it a den of robbers." And when the chief priests and the scribes heard it, they kept looking for a way to kill him. (Mark 11:17–18)

The temple of the heart is a counterpart of the temple to which Jesus made his way on his final arrival in Jerusalem. In theory, as "good Christians" we are unprejudiced people. But we have come to terms with the fact that true hospitality to people of every color, race, and nation is rare, and generally regarded as fantastically idealistic or even treacherously unpatriotic. We learn to conform to that acceptable level of mere toleration that does not antagonize folk around us, and has ample room for all sorts of half-hidden contempt and condescension for "aliens." The open place in the heart where there should be room for the diversity of human beings is crowded with other concerns.

The Spirit strives to make our hearts a house of prayer for all the nations but the resistance we offer is deep-seated and many-sided. To be converted we have to renew our faith in the wisdom of God expressed in creation. "From one ancestor he made all nations to inhabit the whole earth" (Acts 17:26). Human beings are "of one blood," as the King James Version has it. Scorn of men and women of other races and cultures is scorn directed at our own flesh and blood, a venom we inject into our common bloodstream that inevitably poisons our own systems as well as theirs.

We need to meditate on our one blood. We know now that the story of Adam and Eve is a mythical, rather than historical, account of human origins, but that does not mean we should abandon the idea of our single parentage and common origin. In 1987 researchers in molecular biology studying a key set of genes passed on from mother to child down the ages, mitochondrial DNA, came to the conclusion that every person alive today can trace his or her maternal ancestry to one woman who lived in Africa between one hundred thousand and two hundred thousand years ago. This fragment of the story of our mysterious evolution as creatures bearing the divine image and likeness has the power to move us to wonder and to give us a deeper sense of kinship with one another, if we will allow ourselves to meditate upon it in the Spirit. (How often the Creator Spirit must be trying to invite us to meditate upon our new knowledge and pray the unfolding results of the great adventure of scientific research, but we refuse and escape into stale piety!)

We need to cherish our ancestry and the intertwining of our roots. We are the offspring of extraordinary minglings of human beings who have migrated and intermarried in so many complex ways. My own ancestors come from the valleys of Wales, the Pennine hills of the English north-country, and from France. They came also from the steppes of the Ukraine, so thousands of dwellers in towns that have American nuclear missiles aimed at them are my cousins, my people.

We grieve the Spirit within us by our contempt for those of other cultures and races, so we need to consent to the Spirit's exposure of our particular hostilities. Again and again we will discover that what we scorn in certain "aliens" is part of our own selves. We project out of ourselves onto others some aspect of our own beings that we refuse to recognize, let alone revere. Our snubs and contemptuous behavior towards some "foreigners" are ritual attempts to repudiate and rid ourselves of that aspect of our own hearts of which we have made them the representatives and scapegoats. "Blacks" have been and still are the object of oppression by innumerable "whites" who cannot deal with the dark, natural self within and must punish it in the persons of those who have come to symbolize that self. The Spirit in the heart stirs up from the murky depths impulses of scorn and movements of revulsion so that I may face them and repent. Repenting will only go deep if I am prepared to find within myself what the objects of my prejudice have come to represent.

In the creed I affirm my belief in the catholic church. The catholicity of the church is its universal scope as a sacrament of the totality of Christ's redemption. Christ as Son of Man entered into an unconditional solidarity with the whole human race of all times and all places. The new community forged in the ultimate act of identification, the cross, cannot consist of one or two cultures and peoples. It is for all or for none. The church that is called to be a sign of this community and its sacramental embodiment cannot rest until the gifts and the special character of every different race and culture are incorporated into its life, transforming and enriching it. I cannot call myself a catholic Christian unless I embrace this mission.

Spirit of Pentecost, from the beginning you have enabled people of every nation and culture to hear in their own languages the wonderful works of God. You are the inspiration of the church's catholicity.

I am a catholic Christian. Let the word become newly glorious to me. It is not the title of a denomination. It is not the label of a party. It is the sign of my vocation to incarnate the universal embrace of God, the limitless hospitality of God in Christ.

Holy Spirit, it was in your power that the Lord suddenly came to his temple like a refiner's fire. I cannot become in myself a house of prayer for all the nations unless I submit to his work of cleansing. Help me consent to his tearing down within myself the structures of prejudice and narrowness that hinder my witness to the catholicity of the people of God.

MEDITATION
Acts 2

Welcome one another, therefore, just as Christ has welcomed you, for the glory of God. For I tell you that Christ has become a servant of the circumcised on behalf of the truth of God in order that he might confirm the promises given to the patriarchs, and in order that the Gentiles might glorify God for his mercy. As it is written, "Therefore I will confess you

among the Gentiles, and sing praises to your name";
and again he says, "Rejoice, O Gentiles, with his
people"; and again, "Praise the Lord, all you
Gentiles, and let all the peoples praise him"; and
again Isaiah says, "The root of Jesse shall come, the
one who rises to rule the Gentiles; in him the
Gentiles shall hope." May the God of hope fill you
with all joy and peace in believing, so that you may
abound in hope by the power of the Holy Spirit.

Romans 15:7–13

Saturday

WIDOWS' MITES, LIVING STONES

With only a few days to go before the final Passover,
so Mark tells, Jesus spoke to his disciples about the
coming climax of time and history. Every structure that
seemed enduring now would be brought to nothing in a
final act of dissolution and disclosure. Was the temple of
staggering splendor and solidity? Not one stone would be
left standing. Did empires and ancient nations seem
invincible? Wars and tumults would sweep them away. Did
the earth appear secure for ages yet to come? Earthquakes
and disastrous famines would presage its irrevocable decay.
Did the circling stars seems eternal? They would fall too.

The Son of Man would come and gather the elect from the ends of the earth to the ends of heaven. The community of those whom the Son had made his own would be finally revealed as the enduring result of time and history, the new creation to emerge in glory at the last from the ashes of the old.

Mark's church must have cherished this passage, just as the seven churches who received copies of the Revelation to John must have valued them. Little, persecuted communities that seemed so insignificant and fragile in a hostile world drew courage from these great visions of the end. Apocalypse told them that appearances were deceptive. What seemed mighty now—the Roman Empire with its police, the vast mercantile companies, the pagan cult and traditions—God was already beginning to undermine. God's future belonged to the precarious, scattered churches. They had the good news and the new life that would outlast everything else.

The ones who truly hear these passages of scripture are not those who cull literal predictions from them; sectarian "interpreters" of Revelation have repeatedly made the Bible a laughing-stock by the failure of their presumptuous forecasts. The authentic hearers of these words are those who take to heart the truth that appearances are untrustworthy, who look at the world through the eyes of the Spirit of truth. Through these eyes we see, with Mary, that God has already scattered the proud in the imagination of their hearts, put down the mighty from their thrones, exalted those of low degree, filled the hungry with good things and sent the rich empty away. When we use the gift of "the mind of Christ," we see that God has chosen "what is low and despised in the world, things that are not, to reduce to nothing things that are" (1 Corinthians 1:28).

Jesus' teaching about the final reversal, the final disclosure and vindication of God's kingdom that has been hitherto hidden in the world, prepares us for the Passion. The cross reveals how utterly different is the way God works from the methods of the world, The cross reveals that God's wisdom and power work through the foolishness and weakness of suffering love, and therefore remain unrecognized by the "rulers of this age, who are doomed to perish" (1 Corinthians 2:6).

Just before Jesus' apocalyptic teaching, Mark has the story of the widow's mite. We capture the irony of the story better if we use journalistic jargon to entitle it: "Benefactress makes greatest temple donation on record." The point of the story is that appearances are completely misleading. In appearance the rich donors pouring gold coins into the treasury are the generous ones, the pillars and exemplars of religion. The widow slipping in a couple of coppers is beneath notice. She is nobody, her gift is valueless. But Jesus had been sitting opposite and watching. What he sees in the Spirit is the reverse of what the crowd sees. He calls his disciples over to try once more to share with them his vision that penetrates through appearance to the deep structure of God's reality.

> Truly I tell you, this poor widow has put in more than all those who are contributing to the treasury. For all of them have contributed out of their abundance; but she out of her poverty has put in everything she had, all she had to live on. (Mark 12:43–44)

The Spirit in us is striving to form the mind of Christ in us. Having the mind of Christ is revealed in the habit of decoding appearances. Having the mind of Christ, we are conscious of the irony of living in the kingdom of God, an irony which is sometimes delicious and comic, sometimes biting and terrible. The things people take for granted, the things people assume to be real, to be just, to be the "will of God"! To have the mind of Christ is to observe, to watch and pray, to know differently, to be aware of the conflict between the ways of God and the complex of fallen human attitudes and perceptions that Paul called "the flesh."

It is impossible to have a hospitable and compassionate heart without this detachment from appearances, this practice of X-ray vision, using the cross as the lens through which to view people, relationships, events. The mind of the flesh views most people as insignificant and their contributions to life and to God as negligible. It concentrates on celebrities and the influential. With that mind we shut out of our hearts most of neighbors, most of the world.

The Spirit discloses the unique value of each person, admits us to the secret of their place in the heart of God, shows us how even the most obscure and poverty-stricken can enrich the treasury of God with the precious substance of their own life.

After the lesson of the widow's mite, the disciples soon get carried away admiring the magnificent stones of the temple. Jesus tells them that not one will be left standing upon another. After the resurrection their admiration will shift from buildings to the new temple of the Spirit, the living temple of Christ's Body. They will have good news to tell ordinary people, that they are the building blocks of God's dwelling. Each has a place in it, the new temple is incomplete without them, each is needed. And if they protest that they are nobodies, the apostles will tell them that the temple is founded on One who himself was despised and rejected. "The stone that the builders rejected has become the very head of the corner" (1 Peter 2:7).

***

Spirit of God, fill me with the certainty that each person I meet has a place in this new temple in which you dwell. Let me think of each one as potentially a living stone destined to be built into it. There are those I encounter day by day who will not listen to the good news; but the respect I show for their uniqueness and irreplaceable value can prepare a way for the gospel. Sooner or later, on this side of death or the other, they will come face to face with Christ and learn that they too were destined to be built into him. I can at least, poor evangelist as I am, prepare them a little for that moment by honoring them now in the light of the destiny you have helped me to discern.

MEDITATION
Mark 12:41–13:37

Come to him, a living stone, though rejected by mortals yet chosen and precious in God's sight, and like living stones, let yourselves be built into a spiritual house, to be a holy priesthood, to offer spiritual sacrifices acceptable to God through Jesus Christ.

1 Peter 2:4–5

Holy Week

Monday

WHAT WE KNOW

Holy Week is beginning again, and here I am once
more, feeling so unadjusted to it, so utterly inadequate.
Not that "heart of stone" feeling, simply the sense of
being completely out of proportion—something momen-
tous, like the Niagara Falls is thundering down, right
beside me, and there I stand, with a thimble in my hand,
and I'm supposed to dip in and collect something, catch
it up, assimilate it, reacting properly, goodness knows
how. But if you hold a cup under a waterfall, it's not
only knocked right out of your hand, but empty to boot;
the rushing, tumbling water simply rebounds. The only
hope of scooping anything at all is to hold the cup up
carefully at the very edge, under a lost thin trickle.

   This is how it is with me. I'm standing as near as I
can get to the cataract, the thunder and roar of the water
is deafening. I can catch next to nothing and I know
very well that one step nearer and I'll be caught up or
swept away. But maybe this helpless state of just standing aside, this overpowering sense of not being able to do
anything about it is the only sort of adoration I'm
allowed just now. One's eyes closed, turned away—
this, too, is one way of divining the immensity of this

tremendous mystery, of paying reverence, at least, to
something surpassing by far either comprehension or
emotion. When I was young I used to fancy one could
somehow match one's tiny vessel to the onrush from
above by dint of emotional wriggling and writhing.[1]

Every year on this day I read these words from the journals that Ida Görres, a remarkable Catholic writer of
Austrian and Japanese parentage, kept in the 1950s. Some
years I feel overpowered, almost numbed, by what there is
to take in during Holy Week, and in others I have surged
through it preaching and praying with passion. But the
image of the one catching a trickle at the edge of the
waterfall has helped me every year. To feel only inadequacy, to seem overwhelmed by it all, is at least homage to the
enormity of the mystery of the death and resurrection of
the Son. And the most acute insights, and the most powerful proclamation of the Paschal mystery are—even at
their very best—nothing more than droplets from the
cataract. The plenitude of its meaning and force still
eludes me.

The image, though, of the figure bending over the edge
of the falls is a solitary one and as such cannot take too
much weight. It is not as individuals that we pass through
the Paschal mystery year by year but as a community of
faith. Looking at the few drops in my cup—which is all I
can gather of the truth of God-with-us suffering, dying,
and rising—should make me think of all that my co-
believers, my brothers and sisters throughout the world,
are gathering. By myself I know so little; together we know
so much of Christ. The knowledge of God that the Spirit
imparts is a corporate knowledge. What I myself do not
yet know of the divine power and wisdom in the folly of
the cross, my sisters and brothers the world over are coming to know in the crucibles of suffering. Mysteriously,
through the communion of the Holy Spirit, I am entitled

to claim as mine what they through their suffering and faith have brought up from the depths of their experience.

God forbid then that I should treat Holy Week as the backdrop for private musings about my life with Christ. Of all times this is when I should know myself a pilgrim among pilgrims, a limb of the Body, and open my heart to those countless believers to whom the Spirit has and is revealing, through pain and prayer, "what no eye has seen, nor ear heard, nor the human heart conceived, what God has prepared for those who love him" (1 Corinthians 2:9).

What I so far have been allowed to know of Christ crucified and risen is only a trace of what we have known and are coming to know together as a church. Today then I must let my imagination loose to envisage how some of my sisters and brothers the world over are worshiping and struggling. Christians in Latin America are gathering in village schoolrooms to hear the story and celebrate the eucharist not knowing whether guerrillas or government forces will tear them apart next week. Others are singing in jails, wondering whether this will be the year of their release. Some are rejoicing in packed churches after years of persecution in countries blighted by Stalinism. Those who live with poverty beyond my imagining are praising Christ who became poor for their sakes that they might become rich. Millions whose faith has been tested through suffering are taking their anonymous places in churches, carrying silently in their hearts their knowledge that the Risen One with the pierced hands has kept them company in the worst that can befall humankind.

The Spirit has been leading me into truth this Lent. Just now I need to worship the Spirit and give thanks for all the truth into which my sisters and brothers the world over have been entering at the same time; what a vast ocean of experience of God, what depths have been sounded! In the Spirit this is a single great movement of experienced revelation, and my own steps, small as they are, are part of it.

I say "the world over," but what all living believers are coming to know in the struggle of their daily lives of faith is still only seen "in a mirror, dimly." Those whose death has released them into the presence of God have been shown the fullness of the mystery of the cross and resurrection of which we only have glimpses and fragments. Today I am going to think of them, and my own death. Only death can hollow out in me a space great enough to contain the truth as it is in Jesus. Because I still live, my capacity to take him in and grasp the cross is limited. In the end I will need to be undone by death and remade if I am to know fully what God has done through him, and who he is.

Spirit of truth, take from me the ignorance and self-centeredness that imagines that what I know of Christ crucified and risen is all there is to know. Let me cherish what I know, and strive to know more with your help as I worship him once more this Good Friday and Easter. But open the eyes of faith within me to take in the vastness of what the Body in all its countless members is coming to know, and help me appreciate the richness of our corporate experience of Christ, which is too immense to be contained within the vessel of one individual's life. Today I pray for all my brothers and sisters on the same journey in Christ as myself. Together we know him.

MEDITATION

Love never ends. But as for prophecies, they will come to an end; as for tongues, they will cease; as for knowledge, it will come to an end. For we know only in part, and we prophesy only in part; but when the complete comes, the partial will come to an end. When I was a child, I spoke like a child, I thought like a child, I reasoned like a child; when I became an adult, I put an end to childish ways. For now we see in a mirror, dimly, but then we will see face to face. Now I know only in part; then I will know fully, even as I have been fully known. And now faith, hope, and love abide, these three; and the greatest of these is love.

1 Corinthians 13:8–13

Tuesday

POURING THE OINTMENT

If your church follows the custom during Holy Week of reading the passion narratives dramatically, with different voices for the various characters and the congregation taking on the role of the crowd, then you will know how disturbing it is to cry out in church, "Crucify him! Crucify him!" There is a deep wisdom in the practice because it helps us give some expression to our inarticulate knowledge that the rejection, abandonment, betrayal, and execution of Jesus was not something "they" did. They indeed did it, but the whole truth is not uttered until we also say *we* did it. Politicians and ecclesiastics making judgments based on expediency, crowds lusting for scapegoats for their frustrations, disciples saving their own skins, the traitor handing over the hero who has let him down, all these have their counterparts within us. "Look! He is coming with the clouds; every eye will see him, even those who pierced him; and on his account all the tribes of the earth will wail" (Revelation 1:7). By "those who pierced him" scripture does not refer to the executioners alone, who knew not what they did, but to every eye in all the tribes of the earth, you and me.

Yet there are others in the story of the Passion who do not betray or abandon Jesus. What of them? Most of them are women. The woman who anointed Jesus, the "many other women who had come up with him to Jerusalem" (Mark 15:41), the women of Jerusalem who wept for him, the women who stood by him with his mother as he died in torture, the women who tended his dead body and witnessed his burial. Only the disciple whom Jesus loved shares their faithfulness.

In Mark's gospel the woman who anointed Jesus in the house of Simon the leper at Bethany is not named. In John's gospel the disciple whom Jesus loved, who stood with Mary at the foot of the cross, is not named. Perhaps they have no names so that we can each lend them our own. We are not only those who spurn the love of God; we are also those who accept it and return it. Can you identify yourself with these two, as well as with those who colluded to kill Jesus?

During these past forty days we have been letting the scriptures give us images for the conflicts that take place among the selves of the self, and the story of the woman anointing the head of Jesus with precious ointment is yet another story of conflict. The woman is immediately despised for her action. The indignant critics condemn her for senseless waste: that stuff of hers should have been donated for the relief of the poor instead of being emptied over Jesus' head. The voices are pragmatic, moralistic, high-toned. It is difficult to read the critics' words without seeming to hear the scorn that upright men reserve for "the sort of women" who would buy this kind of luxurious oriental cosmetic in the first place, let alone drench the Master in its overpowering scent; how inappropriate, what bad taste! Jesus, with the oil trickling down all over him, springs to her defense. "Let her alone; why do you trouble her? She has done a beautiful thing to me" (Mark 14:6, RSV).

The critics see only a frivolous and meaningless gesture. Jesus experiences it as rich with meaning, gracious, grave, and truthful. She is saluting him magnificently as the one getting ready to die for all. "She has anointed my body beforehand for its burial." She is also being extremely provocative, because the anointing of the head is the ritual conferring royalty; Messiah means anointed one. No one is proclaiming Jesus as Messiah openly. No one has anointed him as the Messiah of God. Silently she comes to the leper's house with her perfume and she takes it upon herself to act as priest and prophet and anoint Jesus' head. Her action was daring in the extreme, too daring for John, who tells an altered story of Mary anointing Jesus' feet, not his head, and for Luke, who omits it from his account of the final days.

Jesus promised that the story would be told in memory of her throughout the world wherever the good news would be preached. In fact she has actually become part of the good news. Part of the good news is that the human heart is not totally depraved, but has within it a wellspring of worship, a place in which Christ is recognized for who he truly is, a place where courage rises up in love no matter what conventions are disturbed, where there is a flame of generosity and response to grace.

This woman breaking open her costly flask appears again and again in stories of faith. She has inspired artists in their creation of works that glorify God in wood, stone, paint, gesture, movement, melody, and thread, while the pious sneered that these things were unnecessary, wasteful, impractical, and unspiritual. She has inspired men and women following the Spirit's call to monastic life, to make adoration their reason for being, when their friends and family complained that they were wasting their lives. She has smiled upon thousands who tend the flame of prayer and love of Jesus in the midst of busy lives, when those around them view their devotion as wasted effort diverting them from achievement and doing good. Her memory has been present like a fragrance in thousands of bold responses to Jesus in the face of condescension and disapproval.

Spirit of truth, how far from simple is the whole truth of who I am as you draw me once again into the solemn re-experiencing of Jesus' death and resurrection. On the one hand I must cry "Crucify him!" with my fellow worshipers, and sing "'Twas I, Lord Jesus, I it was denied thee: I crucified thee." On the other hand I must not let hallowed phrases like "there is no health in us" lead me astray. There is health in me, because you are in me blowing into flame the spark of love for Christ! I can use the sense of sinfulness and impotence as a shelter for mediocrity and a pretext for not nurturing that person within me that the woman who anointed Jesus represents so wonderfully. Spirit of beauty, because you are alive in me I can delight Jesus with beautiful actions as she did. I can be extravagant with my time, in prayer and in worship, and defy the voices that accuse this extravagance as pointless and indulgent. With you moving in my heart I can throw away some of the inhibitions that restrain me from letting go in wonder, love, and praise.

MEDITATION

While he was at Bethany in the house of Simon the leper, as he sat at the table, a woman came with an alabaster jar of very costly ointment of nard, and she broke open the jar and poured the ointment on his head. But some were there who said to one another in anger, "Why was the ointment wasted in this way? For this ointment could have been sold for more than three hundred denarii, and the money given to the poor." And they scolded her. But Jesus said, "Let her alone; why do you trouble her? She has performed a good service for me. For you always have the poor with you, and you can show kindness to them whenever you wish; but you will not always have me. She has done what she could; she has anointed my body beforehand for its burial. Truly I tell you, wherever the good news is proclaimed in the whole world, what she has done will be told in remembrance of her."

Mark 14:3–9

You may feel drawn to identify yourself with the unnamed woman and let the story unfold in your heart. Relive her feelings, experience Jesus' reactions, pray what you feel.

Wednesday

LYING CLOSE TO THE BREAST OF JESUS

Pictures of the last supper tend to show a certain awkwardness in depicting the disciple whom Jesus loved lying close to his breast. He seems to lean towards Jesus at an odd angle. I suppose the simple reason is that most pictures show everyone sitting up around a table, whereas the phrase in John's gospel presupposes that the disciples are reclining for the meal. Lying down on his side, the disciple closest to Jesus had only to lean back a little and his head would be against Jesus' chest. Yet with uncanny faithfulness the awkwardness of the pictures expresses the mixed feelings and embarrassment many people feel about the beloved disciple. Preachers do not often mention him and those who read the Bible are often nonplussed when they come across the passages that refer to him.

If we are pressed we might admit that we are disconcerted by the idea that Jesus had a favorite companion. Shouldn't Jesus have regarded everyone equally? Our ideal picture of him is of one who would be "just the same" towards all his disciples. We are displeased that John's gospel contradicts our ideal of fairness. And we are distressed to think of Jesus needing the intimacy of a particular friendship. Shouldn't the Son of God have been above needing the solace of a special companion? Doesn't that need show him to be too vulnerable for our liking? Friendship has not always been valued in Christianity, and many people who have been conditioned to "suspect the worst" of deep intimacy between people of the same sex are likely to feel especially uneasy contemplating this scene of physical and personal closeness between Jesus and the disciple he loved.

If we are puzzled by the place this man had in Jesus' life, so was Peter, according to the closing words of John's gospel. Peter is curious about how the beloved disciple's life will unfold now after the resurrection:

> Peter turned and saw the disciple whom Jesus loved following them; he was the one who had reclined next to Jesus at the supper and had said, "Lord, who is it that is going to betray you?" When Peter saw him, he said to Jesus, "Lord, what about him?" Jesus said to him, "If it is my will that he remain until I come, what is that to you? Follow me!" (John 21:20–22)

The beloved disciple's role is not pastoral leadership like Peter's. He will simply remain. This is the same word translated elsewhere in the gospel as "abide." He will bear witness to the mystery of abiding in Christ. He will show what it means to live in response to the invitation, "Abide in me as I abide in you" (John 15:4).

Perhaps the disciple is never named, never individualized, so that we can more easily accept that he bears witness to an intimacy that is meant for each one of us. The closeness he enjoyed is a sign of the closeness that is mine and yours because we are in Christ and Christ is in us.

I am called to live, I am called to pray, "close to the breast of Jesus." There is no one and no thing between me and the heart of Christ. The gospel of John uses the same image to express the mystery that there was no one and no thing between Jesus and the Father. "No one has ever seen God. It is God the only Son, who is close to the Father's heart, who has made him known" (John 1:18). I am right up against the heart of Christ when I pray; and Christ is right in the bosom of God.

Today in the middle of Holy Week I can take to heart what it would cost to allow myself to experience fully this intimacy that is already mine. Closeness to Jesus at the supper was not a matter of affectionate reverie. The heart whose beat the beloved disciple could hear was pounding in anticipation of arrest, degradation, and death by torture: Jesus "was troubled in spirit." The conversation he was uniquely placed to have with Jesus was about the treachery of one of the twelve. Abiding with Jesus meant standing by the cross with Mary and the other women, exposed to the full horror of his brutal execution.

To live close to the heart of Jesus would mean living in contact with the joy and the agony of Christ. It is not possible to have one without the other. If in prayer I simply allowed myself to be loved instead of talking so much, I would enter into the joy of Christ. In contemplation the Spirit of love—which flows forth from the Father into and over Christ and flows from him in return to the Father— would be coursing through my being. But if I allowed myself to enjoy the simplicity of that closeness, I would be close enough to sense the pain of God, too. The divine pain at the world's, your, my incessant rejection of divine love, our indifference and ingratitude, cruelty, sham, and pomp.

The heart of Christ was pierced by a spear thrust into his side, and the Risen Christ has a terrible wound which cannot be healed as long as time runs on. "Reach out your hand and put it in my side. Do not doubt but believe" (John 20:27). Prayer would mean compunction, grief, lament, feeling with the pain of a rejected and despised God.

To live close to the heart of Christ with its abounding joy and terrible pain would mean keeping contact with the joy and pain of those in whom he lives. The disciple whom Jesus loved was the first to recognize him in the shadowy form of a stranger on the lakeshore tending a little fire on the beach. To abide in Christ is to stay with and in him in the life he lives identified with everyone everywhere. He is in all the strangers, all my neighbors. Abiding in him, staying close to his heart, means being open to their joys and sorrows. My mystical union with him comes down to the everyday task of weeping with those who weep and rejoicing with those who rejoice.

Spirit of Christ, water from the side of Christ, you are the life of his Heart. You live in my heart and long to be its life. You are the living bond, the vital link, the shared life that enables me to live "heart to heart" with Christ.

I ask you to make me less afraid of being in touch with his joy and his pain. Especially I ask to be more open to the joy and pain of the members of his Body, my neighbors, the strangers with whom I have to do. You can wear down the illusion that they are aliens with whom I need to have little to do. You can help me weep and rejoice with them, enter into solidarity with them in Christ.

Spirit of God, convince me that I am the disciple whom Jesus loves. Only by knowing more deeply that he loves me will you overcome my fear that living so closely to him will be more than I can bear. Love knows what I can bear.

MEDITATION
John 13:21–30

What if you were to put yourself in the place of the beloved disciple in the account of the last supper and experience the event through his eyes? What feelings and thoughts might arise? What would it be like to express those feelings to Christ?

Maundy Thursday

IF I DO NOT
WASH YOU

In retreats I have asked many people to meditate on the scene of the foot-washing, imagining themselves as one of the participants, so that they could pray out of the feelings that arise from experiencing the event. A few of them have identified themselves with Jesus or with Judas but most are drawn to being Peter. Who knows what the other disciples felt when they looked down at Jesus at their feet? Peter, though, was honest enough not to pretend that he could tolerate it. Again and again I hear retreatants say how Peter's horror uncovered their own. It is one thing to took up to Jesus in prayer as Master and Lord. It is altogether another thing to look down at him, to see him looking up at me and to allow him to wash my feet.

Feeling in the meditation with Peter this intense reluctance to be washed by Jesus is a precious revelation that can bring us to the heart of the matter of the cross. "You do not know now what I am doing, but later you will understand" (John 13:7). Only after the crucifixion arid resurrection can the foot-washing he seen as a symbol interpreting in advance the outpouring of unconditional love on the cross. "Having loved his own who were in the world, he loved them to the end" (John 13:1). The Son does a slave's work at the dinner table, before dying a slave's death to show the lengths to which God will go to reconcile us. The symbolic act brings to the surface our reactions to the love of God on the cross. The reluctance to be served humbly by Jesus the servant, the revulsion at his uncovering our filthy feet and washing them tenderly, is an unveiling of the resistance we will bring to Calvary where the one who took the form of a servant "humbled himself and became obedient to the point of death—even death on a cross" (Philippians 2:8).

The foot-washing throws light on how the cross judges us. The issue is whether we will accept absolute and unconditional love and allow it to envelop and penetrate us wholly. After Jesus has demeaned himself in washing their feet, Judas's disgust with him becomes total and he goes out into the night to betray him. The mystery of damnation is the possibility deep in the heart of every human being of totally repudiating the embrace of divine Love in a final "No." During the foot-washing Peter has to face his resistance to being served. The mystery of salvation is the possibility in the heart of every human being of overcoming our dread of unconditional love and consenting with a yielding "Yes" to its victory over our shame and the healing of our alienation.

Though foot-washing belongs to other eras and climates than our own, the symbol can still resonate enough to disturb and provoke. When are we washed? As helpless babies, we are washed by our mothers, on whose love we are totally dependent. When we are sick and unable to move, by nurses to whose care we must entrust ourselves. Otherwise never, except as part of the reciprocal pleasure of bathing with lovers. Letting another wash us raises the issue of dependence and entrusting ourselves completely to the touch and care of another's hands. The atonement of the cross brings us to a place where we must either accept being entirely receptive or flee to preserve our craving to be in control ourselves. God alone can do what must be done. God alone can overcome the separation, demolish the barrier, fill in the lack, annihilate the debt. "While we were still weak, at the right time Christ died for the ungodly" (Romans 5:6).

"Unless I wash you, you have no share with me" (John 13:8). There is no sentimentality in Jesus as he looks up at us with his basin and towel. His words are strong and leave no room for compromise. Today, on Maundy Thursday, in preparation for tomorrow, he asks us to face the danger that our reluctance to be served puts us in. If we will not allow him to serve us, then we cut ourselves off from him.

If we will let the Spirit draw us into its depths, this moment of truth between Peter and Jesus can show us what our human fallenness is. At some unnameable moment in the early days of emergence into personhood, each one of us reenacts a fateful bargain to rid ourselves of the hope of being loved absolutely. It is as though we make some decision at a level deeper than consciousness to go it alone, to earn love on our own terms, to buy it from others, or to replace it with gratification from things or our own endeavors. But the amputation of the God-implanted hope never quite works. There is the "feel of a lost limb cut off in another life." Jesus comes to us bearing all the unnerving signs of life lived within the embrace of unconditional love. He attacks the bargain we made, undermines our craven great refusal, inflames our hope to be loved absolutely by the Father of all, tests it in the ordeal of dereliction and abandonment on the cross, vindicates it in his shocking resurrection.

Peter is jolted by Jesus' stern words. "Lord, not my feet only but also my hands and my head!" (John 13:9). But his own reluctance to being reduced to helplessness cannot be canceled except through the shattering of his heroism in his threefold denial of Jesus.

On Maundy Thursday it is good to abandon the pretense that there is no vestige left in us of resistance to being served and loved. I am a Christian. I have accepted the love of God on the cross...and yet there is a reluctance which has not altogether died down in me yet. Part of me wants to deserve love, or only get the love I deserve. I do not mind exchanging gifts, but being only and entirely on the receiving end does not sit well with me. There is evidence from my prayer life: how often do I look down at Jesus in prayer and consent to his washing away the daily grime of my frustrations, struggles, mistakes? I prefer to try to do it for myself.

Spirit of yielding, Spirit of consent, Spirit of Yes, Spirit of letting-go, Spirit of acceptance, Spirit of humility and openness, Spirit who trains my eyes to look down at Jesus looking up to me, ever ready to wash and serve me—I need you. I need you to give me a fresh receptivity to the unconditional love of God, to make my embrace of the cross real and not just a matter of words.

MEDITATION
Romans 5

Good Friday

NUMBERED
WITH THE
TRANSGRESSORS

*"I have a baptism with which to be baptized, and what
stress I am under until it is completed!" (Luke 12:50)*

Jesus faced the prospect of his arrest and execution with
a mixture of dread and of agonized yearning. In his baptism in the Jordan he had bound himself to suffering and
struggling humanity; but only in his death could he show
the magnitude of his identification with us in our alienation. Only by dying numbered with the transgressors as a
disgraced criminal on a slave's cross could he show that his
embrace of us had no limits and no exceptions. He had to
abandon in the end every shred of credibility as a holy
wonder-worker in the destruction of his movement, and
by publicly submitting to torture that would lead him into
the annihilating darkness of the godless. "My God, my
God, why have you forsaken me?" (Mark 15:34).

He had asked James and John: "Are you able to drink
the cup that I drink, or be baptized with the baptism that
I am baptized with?" (Mark 10:38)—then he promised

them they would. He asks the same question of us. If we allow his cross to work its way with us there is a baptism of fire we have to undergo, a baptism into solidarity with sinners. We build up our false selves on the principle that we are right and good enough; evil lies outside us, incarnated in "them," villains and criminals, whores and vixens, rebels and addicts. To abandon this principle is tantamount to consenting to the dismantling of the very structure of our selves. If "I" and "them" should give way to "we," then a new self with a new center would have to be found. The cross kills the old self that was based on the fiction that the others are the guilty.

Every Good Friday we return to the foot of the cross to reexpose ourselves to the devastating and glorious absurdity that Paul could only express in the bizarre words, "For our sake [God] made him to be sin who knew no sin" (2 Corinthians 5:21). Christ brought his sinlessness into identification with our sin. Words fail us, but as we gaze on the incandescent mystery it acts like radiation therapy, searching out and burning away those newly formed places within ourselves where the cancerous lie that the others are the needy and the guilty has reestablished itself since the last treatment. We are all one in our guilt, we are all one in our need, we are all one in the embrace of a suffering God, we are all one as heirs of the gift of a new self, offered in the resurrection.

He was numbered with the transgressors, crucified between the thieves. We will not find him in our hearts except in the same company. For each Good Friday to be good the Spirit must take us by the hand and reestablish our contact with that inmost core of recalcitrant evil, enmity, and impotence where we are sisters and brothers of the most depraved and lost. That is where Christ is, clasping them with his pierced hands.

Today, though my time should be mostly spent "lost in wonder, love, and praise," I need to clear a little space to look back over the last year and check what it has meant for me to take up my cross and follow him. Taking up the cross means leaving the company of the good for the company of the condemned. Why else were the Romans' victims made to carry the crossbar of their instruments of torture, except to advertise their criminality to the populace? I take up the cross and follow Jesus whenever I acknowledge my oneness with the guilty, whenever I stop pretending that they are an alien class. I put the cross down and hide among the moral crowd whenever I gloat over the sins of others; whenever I thank God that I am not as other men are; even when I say: "There but for the grace of God go I"; whenever I resort to all the tools of projection to distance myself from the chaotic and the bad. The extent to which I have taken up the cross will be shown by the frequency and intensity of my prayers for sinners, enemies, and the lost as my brothers and sisters, my own flesh. Which means that I have hardly begun to take up my cross.

In prayer I must practice being numbered among the transgressors and must start to care for this company where I belong. I remind myself of the wonderful exemplar of the messy passion of true intercession in Flannery O'Connor's short story *Greenleaf*. Mrs. Greenleaf is the slatternly tenant of the prim Mrs. May who disapproves of her bitterly because she neglects her house in order to practice her prayer healing.

> She cut all the morbid stories out of the newspaper—the accounts of women who had been raped and criminals who had escaped and children who had been burned and of train wrecks and plane crashes and the divorces of movie stars. She took these to the woods and dug a hole and buried them and then she fell on the ground over them.... She groaned "Jesus, Jesus"... her legs and arms spread out as if she were trying to wrap them round the earth.[2]

I take as my examples again those monks among whom George Bernanos, the great Catholic novelist, was once staying when he was agonized by a newspaper account of the arrest of a mass murderer. He was driven to write to the man's lawyer to express to her the feelings that had rent his heart to the point of agony

> and beyond agony, because it is heart-rending in that there is in it a hope that one can scarcely conceive of: the solidarity of all men in Christ.... As far as I am concerned I have nothing much to offer him. I would like him to be able to understand that there are monks, lonely like him, who do better than just pity him, but who will from now on take over, as brothers should, part of his appalling burden.[3]

Spirit of Christ, the beloved disciple saw in the pouring out of water with the blood from Jesus' pierced side your outpouring. You are the Spirit of self-giving love, you are the Spirit of reconciliation, you are the Spirit who binds us in one, you come to us from the smitten rock of Christ. Only if you pour anew from him within my heart will this Good Friday be good for me—and for those whom I have the power to touch while I live. Because only by a fresh drinking in of your power will I really grasp the solidarity of all in him, and begin to play my part once more of pouring out his compassion over the needy, the desperate, the separated, the hardened, the hopeless, the unforgiven, all those living lives of quiet desperation. . . .

MEDITATION

> "Take hold of yourself and make yourself responsible for all men's sins. My friend, believe me, that really

179

is so, for the moment you make yourself responsible in all sincerity for everyone and everything, you will see that it really is so and that you are in fact responsible for everyone and everything."[4]

Father Zossima in The Brothers Karamazov

Holy Saturday

HE DESCENDED
INTO HELL

The last of the forty days is one of silence. There is no eucharist today, no preaching. The church puts a finger to her lips. Words do not work very well when it comes to the mystery of Christ dead, the death of God-with-us. To be silent in awe is different, though, from being mute out of ignorance. We know something about today and what it means, though what we know can hardly be put into words. Holy Saturday is silent not because it is a mere hiatus before the resurrection like sleep, but because today we are asked to take our imaginations to their breaking-point in following Jesus to the utmost limit of his solidarity with us.

Scripture tells us that by joining all the dead in their deadness, Jesus gave them access to the new community of love that would spring into life with his resurrection.

For Christ also suffered for sins once for all, the
righteous for the unrighteous, in order to bring you
to God. He was put to death in the flesh, but made
alive in the spirit, in which also he went and made
a proclamation to the spirits in prison, who in for-
mer times did not obey, when God waited patiently
in the days of Noah, during the building of the ark,
in which a few, that is eight persons, were saved
through water. (1 Peter 3:18–20)

The words have the awkwardness of someone struggling to
contain a vast truth in an implausible, inadequate vessel.
The writer takes us back to Genesis and the despair of
God over a hopelessly unresponsive mass of humanity.

The LORD saw that the wickedness of humankind
was great in the earth, and that every inclination of
the thoughts of their hearts was only evil continually. And the LORD was sorry that he had made
humankind on the earth, and it grieved him to his
heart. (Genesis 6:5–6)

From the population of the world, only eight can be sal-
vaged. The rest are wiped out as beyond redemption.

But the word of the cross is that no one and no thing is
beyond the reach of redemption in Christ. So the writer
paints a mythic image of strangely moving power. The
multitudes of the disobedient dead whom God abandoned
in disgust are in the vast prison of Hades. Christ through
his own death joins the dead, but as the herald of their liberation. They are not excluded from union with God. The
new reconciled community is meant to include them too.

Orthodox icons of the resurrection show Christ in his
glory trampling on the unhinged and broken doors of
Hades. With one hand he pulls up Adam from the nether
darkness, and with the other Eve. They express something
that western pictures of a solitary Christ ascending from
his own grave do not. Gazing on these icons, we are irra-

diated with the truth that we have been, are being, and only will be saved together with one another. "As all die in Adam, so all will be made alive in Christ....so that God may be all in all" (1 Corinthians 15:22, 28).

The theme of Christ's penetration of the abode of the dead gave rise in western Christianity to the dramatic myth of the harrowing of hell. It moves me to think of the medieval craftsmen who would attempt, as part of the cycle of mystery plays, to show the triumphant Christ, bursting into the torture chambers of the devils of hell and robbing the fiends of their victims. Grotesque we find them, but I feel that these men, stamping around in their ludicrous costumes, knew something that the pedantic teachers of my youth did not, with their reminders that the phrase in the creed "he descended into hell" really meant only that he joined the deceased. Now, as the third millennium begins, the words "he descended into hell" are more needful to us than ever before. In our time we have seen hell on earth, and it is far more terrible than the worst dreams of medieval carvers and painters. We have seen hell in the death camps of Nazi Germany and Cambodia, in Hiroshima. The mouths of hell are as close to us now as the streets of El Salvador and the tastefully landscaped research facilities for biological warfare in our countryside.

Today I will in silence make these words my own: "He descended into hell." There is no place that can shut out the "love of God in Christ Jesus our Lord." No human heart or community—however eaten up with corruption and violence, however consumed with loathing or committed to death—no inner or outer hell can hold out ultimately against the penetrating and life-giving power of this death and resurrection. There is no place in me, however dead, however false, out of his reach. Through the mystery of my own undoing in death every last and lost part of me will be opened up to his life-giving Spirit and brought within the embrace of our Father.

In these forty days we have been "practicing the scales of rejoicing," allowing the Spirit who is alive within us to show us a little more of our self, more of our many selves that make each one of us a microcosm of the humanity God is healing through Christ. "Bless the LORD, O my soul, and all that is within me, bless his holy name" (Psalm 103:1). The Spirit of truth has helped us to realize a little better the diversity each one of us encompasses in the heart, what a world is meant by the words "all that is within me." The Spirit has acted as the Advocate of some of the conflicted, gifted, wounded, imprisoned, banished, beautiful, desiring, lost, angry, fearful, creative selves whom we are usually so reluctant to face, but among whom Christ lives and acts as Savior of all. By showing us how Christ touches each self of my self the Spirit has helped empower us some more to act as the agents of his touch for others.

Spirit of new life, breathed into me from the Risen Christ, prepare me to celebrate his rising in your power. Something has happened on the first day of the week, powerful enough to heal every wound, to recover every waste, to break down every barrier, to unlock every prison, to forgive every transgression, to unite everything at odds. There is love enough to flood every heart, to raise everyone dead and lost . . . but this is too much for me to grasp and, without your help, overwhelmed by the immensity of it all, I will be tempted to shrink the resurrection to the proportions of my own understanding and my Easter will be worldly and banal. Help me to lose myself in adoration. I cannot grasp the resurrection. But it can grasp me and give rise in me to a loving heart that is losing the limits of its compassion.

MEDITATION
Psalm 116   Romans 8:28–39

ENDNOTES

The Beginning of Lent
1. Dorothy L. Sayers, *Gaudy Night* (London: Gollancz, 1935), 322.

The First Week of Lent
1. Quoted in Hans Urs von Balthasar, *The Glory of the Lord* (San Francisco and New York: Ignatius/Crossroads, 1983), 404.
2. Isaac the Syrian, *Ascetical Homilies* 81:51. Compare the translation published by Holy Transfiguration Monastery, Boston, Mass., 1984.
3. *Homilies of St. Macarius*, quoted in *The Art of Prayer*, ed. Timothy Ware (London: Faber and Faber, 1966), 18-19.
4. e. e. cummings, χαιρε (New York: Liveright, 1979), 11.
5. St. Peter Damian, *Selected Writings on the Spiritual Life*, trans. Patricia McNulty (London: Faber, 1959), 57.
6. Carl Jung, *Modern Man in Search of a Soul* (London: K. Paul, Trench, Trubner, 1936), 271.

The Second Week of Lent
1. Quoted in *Thomas Merton: Monk*, ed. Patrick Hart (New York: Sheed and Ward, 1974), 80.
2. Nicolas Berdyaev, *The Destiny of Man* (London: Bles, 1937), 156.
3. Thomas Merton, *Cistercian Studies*, vol. IX (1974), 59.
4. Dag Hammarskjöld, *Markings* (London: Faber, 1964), 110.

The Third Week of Lent

1. Frank O'Connor, *Collected Stories* (New York: Vintage Books, 1982), 479.
2. Rowan Williams, *The Wound of Knowledge* (London: Darton, Longman and Todd, 1979), 11.
3. Meister Eckhart, *Breakthrough: Meister Eckhart's Creation Spirituality in New Translation*, introduction and commentaries by Matthew Fox (New York: Garden City, 1980), 111.
4. Julien Green, *Vers L'Invisible* (Paris: Plon, 1967), 238.
5. Isaac the Syrian, *Sentences*, quoted in Paul Evdokimov, *The Struggle with God* (Glen Rock, N.J.: Paulist Press, 1966), 103, 216.
6. Lorenzo Scupoli, *Unseen Warfare*, trans. G. E. H. Palmer and E. Kadloubovsky (London: Faber and Faber, 1963).
7. Thomas Merton, *Conjectures of a Guilty Bystander* (Garden City, N.Y.: Doubleday, 1966), 128, 12.

The Fourth Week of Lent

1. Quoted in Laurens van der Post, *Jung and the Story of Our Time* (London: Hogarth, 1976), 123.
2. Robert Kegan, *The Evolving Self* (Cambridge: Harvard University Press, 1982), 20.
3. Charles Péguy, "A Prayer in Confidence," in *Charles Péguy: The Mystery of the Holy Innocents etc.*, trans. Pansy Pakenham (London: Harvill Press, 1956), 35.

Holy Week

1. Ida Friederike Görres, *Broken Lights* (London: Burns Oates, 1960), 77.
2. Flannery O'Connor, *Everything That Rises Must Converge* (New York: Farrar, Straus & Giroux, 1956), 30f.
3. George Bernanos, *Correspondence*, vol. 2 (Paris: Plon, 1971), quoted in R. Zaehner, *Our Savage God* (London: Collins, 1974), 303.
4. Feodor Dostoevsky, *The Brothers Karamazov*, vol. I (London: Penguin, 1958), 376–77.

A GUIDE FOR
PRAYING WITH
SCRIPTURE

You may find these classic ways of praying with scripture helpful in meditating on suggested passages.

Entering Into Stories
1) Spend a few moments settling down. Say a prayer such as the collect for purity (BCP 355) slowly. Then ask God to touch you through the passage of scripture and give you the experience of grace that you need at this time.
2) Read the story slowly and carefully several times, pausing between each reading for half a minute or so until the episode takes hold of you. Let the details of the story emerge. Let questions and insights occur as you notice more with each reading.
3) Put the Bible aside. Now sink into the scene. Let it come to life with you as a participant. Do not look at it as if it were a film projected onto a screen. In your imagination take part in it. Notice the details, let yourself see, hear, and smell the scene. Let yourself be one of the people caught up in the action, such as Peter, or Mary Magdalen, or the sick person Christ intends to heal, or one of the bystanders.

4) Let the drama slowly unfold. Let what happens, happen. Do not control the story. Let yourself feel what happens and do not moralize by trying to glean lessons from the story, or attempt to wring teachings or clever applications from it. Allow yourself to be affected by the words and actions of the story.

5) As your feelings are affected by the event, let yourself express these feelings to Christ. How does this touch your life? What do you feel moved to ask for or to give thanks for? Or just stay with the impression the story has had on you, savoring it and soaking yourself in it in the presence of the Lord in silent awareness, or with the gentle repetition of a single word or phrase from the story.

Holy Reading

This form of prayer is ideal for the many passages of scripture that are not narratives, such as the psalms, the epistles, and the teaching sections in the gospels.

1) Spend a few moments settling down and pray that your heart may be open and attentive to the gift God knows you need today.

2) Begin reading the passage very slowly indeed with an open mind. Do not study the text, simply read slowly.

3) When a particular sentence or phrase or single word "lights up" or "rings a bell" or seems striking, inviting, or claims your attention, put the Bible down. Resist the temptation to go on. Here the reading stops and the meditation begins.

4) Gently repeat this phrase or word again and again. Do not attempt to force any particular meanings from the words. This phase of meditation was compared by the monks of old to the way cows lie down and chew the cud. You know what the words mean, so just savor and relish them by gentle repetition. After some time you may find yourself shortening the sentence to just a few words or even just one. When you feel that you have really absorbed the words and are filled with a particular feeling

or attitude or impression they have evoked, the time has come to lay aside the repetition or meditation phase.

5) Now is the time for prayer. You may begin to express to God what impression the words have made on you. You may want to give thanks for the gift they signify, or question Christ or ask him for something arising from the feelings they have evoked. Keep it simple, praying spontaneously. Or you may want to stay in loving silence in the presence of God, filled with the grace or attitude that the meditation has instilled. When it gets hard to prolong this spontaneous prayer or moment of awareness and distraction sets in, bring the prayer-time gently to a close with a word of thanksgiving.